# FOOTLIGHT DREAMS

## FOLLOWING YOUR PASSION FOR A CAREER IN MUSICAL THEATRE

A Guide for Performers, Parents and Teachers

BY DAVID LADD

ISBN 978-1-61780-464-9

Published by Hal Leonard Corporation
7777 W. Bluemound Road
P.O. Box 13819
Milwaukee, WI 53213

Library of Congress Cataloging-in-Publication Data

Ladd, David, 1962-
  Footlight dreams : following your passion for a career in musical theatre a guide for performers, parents and teachers / by David Ladd. -- 1st ed.
    p. cm.
  ISBN 978-1-61780-464-9
  1. Musical theater--Vocational guidance. 2. Music--Vocational guidance. 3. Acting--Vocational guidance. 4. Dance--Vocational guidance. I. Title.
  ML3795.L145 2012
  792.6'0293--dc23
                              2011036524

Printed in the U.S.A.

First Edition

Visit Hal Leonard Online at **www.halleonard.com**

# FOOTLIGHT DREAMS
## TABLE OF CONTENTS

# ACKNOWLEDGMENTS

The cast of The Actors Fund's 2003 benefit performance of *Chess in Concert* who, although already volunteering their own time and energy to a worthy cause, so graciously filled out my questionnaire.

Ben Cohen and members of the Broadway cast in the revival of *Gypsy*. Ben, I'm proud to claim, was a student from my first teaching job, at Deerfield High School in Deerfield, Illinois, and the first of my former students to perform in a Broadway show.

Larry Raben and members of the Broadway cast of *The Producers*. Larry is one of the kindest and sincerest people I've ever met. The fact that he was willing to persuade twelve busy people from a vigorous, exhausting show to fill out a random survey for someone he'd known only a few weeks speaks volumes about the kind of person he is and dispels the stereotype of the selfish actor.

The entire cast of Westchester Broadway Theatre's *Footloose*. These great people were so supportive of my efforts and willingly offered advice and encouragement that would enhance this project. Although they were my family for only three months, I'll always remember them.

The administration and institution of New Trier High School for having a program in place that encourages teachers to leave the environment, explore, and learn, and then return to share their knowledge and greater understanding of their discipline and the world.

The members of the music department at New Trier High School for giving me the green light to go on the sabbatical and allowing me to come back to lead one of the finest high school music departments in the country.

Paul Castree for his advice regarding the musical theatre business and support of my career—and for allowing me to talk about him in this book!

Phil Smith, a colleague, friend, and mentor, for his wisdom and suggestions with the first draft of this book.

Greg Harris, a colleague and fellow musical theatre admirer, for taking the time to edit the guidebook after its first incarnation. He is greatly missed.

Laura Bertani, Erika Erhart, and Jason Feldman for their vision, creativity, and execution of the first edition of the guidebook.

My family for their continued support of my career and for coming to visit me in New York City!

My talented wife, Katherine Condit-Ladd. Not only did she devote an exorbitant amount of time to endless rereads and editing suggestions but she also supported me in every endeavor leading up to, during, and after the sabbatical leave.

My editor with Hal Leonard, Dulcie Shoener, who added depth to this book by asking compelling questions and who polished my writing so it was ready to share with young performers, teachers, and parents.

Lastly, to Emily Crocker, whose faith in me and this book has given it new life and the opportunity to help many young, talented artists lead promising careers in musical theatre.

To all I am forever grateful.

# BEHIND THE
# *FOOTLIGHT DREAMS* PROJECT

Since I began teaching high school choral music in 1994, I have been asked a multitude of questions about musical theatre as a possible career by a multitude of students. Because I had a background as a professional—my fourteen-year musical theatre career began the summer after my freshman year in college and extended nine years past the bestowing of my bachelor's degree—I have given advice that was fairly soundly based in that experience.

However, I always knew that a lot more useful information was out there and that if I found a way to collect as much as possible, it would only enhance the advice I give and the process my students use to make decisions.

Additionally, I had always wanted to try my hand at living and working in New York City. Goals that had been left behind as I delved into my teaching career—such as getting my Equity card (becoming a union actor) and working on Broadway—remained in the back of my mind. Although I was a little older, I still thought there was a possibility I could achieve these goals.

On the plane ride home from a visit to New York in the summer of 2000, I realized that it was essential for me to attempt the goals before the window of opportunity closed. After some brainstorming, I decided that I could combine two related goals (compiling information for students and pursuing personal performance dreams) in a sabbatical leave from New Trier High School. An additional three years would pass before I could take the leave.

In the summer of 2003, I embarked on a year's sabbatical leave from my position as choral director and Music Department chair at New Trier High School in Winnetka, Illinois. I had two basic goals. The first was to accumulate information about musical theatre as a profession. This information would, in turn, help my students at New Trier who are interested in musical theatre as a career make difficult decisions about schools, majors, and their futures. The second was to resurrect my career as a professional musical theatre actor and see how I would fare in New York City. I expected that the second goal would influence and enhance the first.

The sabbatical project, as originally conceived, had several components:

- A survey for distribution to seventy-five working actors regarding their careers in the field. (The survey was not meant to become a scientifically precise document, but was created and distributed to gather and assess general information and opinions from working actors.)

- Pursuit of the musical theatre career through training (taking dance and acting classes, private voice lessons, and consistent gym workouts), auditioning, and working in the field.

- A journal to be kept for one year, reflecting upon my experience of auditioning, training, and living in NYC.

- A guidebook to help students (and their parents) while deciding on possible career paths. The booklet would be a compilation of all information assembled from the survey and from "wisdom" acquired during my year as an actor in NYC (as well as fourteen years as a musical theatre professional prior to my teaching career).

The guidebook was originally intended for the students of New Trier, but as it began to take shape it seemed that it could benefit students anywhere. It received enthusiastic support from many and I was encouraged to do whatever I could to give it wider distribution.

The original book, with two sections, was compiled into a document titled *Musical Theatre As Career Choice* and received a limited, informal printing in 2005. The first section was the guide for students and parents mentioned above. The second section is directly related to pursuit of a musical theatre career in New York City, and contains relevant data and my own personal reflections and opinions about that experience.

After meeting with Emily Crocker of Hal Leonard Publishing, who saw potential in the book, I was encouraged to add a third section for teachers. It can be used to engage students in thought-provoking dialogue and help them make wise decisions about the career. The third section seemed like the missing ingredient that could maximize the distribution of the book, getting it into the hands (and heads) of as many musical-theatre-professionals-to-be as possible.

I hope this book will be a useful tool in the difficult process of planning for the future. Choosing musical theatre as a career can be a scary proposition, but when you are armed with knowledge, a smart choice is achievable.

Break a leg!

*David Ladd*

# part one

## A GUIDE FOR PERFORMERS, PARENTS AND TEACHERS

# SECTION ONE:
# A Preposterous Idea

## QUOTES FROM THE PROS TO SCARE YOU OFF

When you ask seventy-five Broadway pros for advice they'd give to young people dreaming about a career in musical theatre, the answers will either scare you off or make you stronger.

*"If theatre is what you need, want, and love to do, then go ahead. The lifestyle is too difficult. Relationships are strained. Holidays disappear. If you want to live 'normally' then choose something else."*

*"Playing well with others means doing your job 100 percent each and every day and each and every performance. If you're in the business to 'be famous,' I suggest a different route. If you want to be a skilled performer and have a successful career (which means working steadily at your craft), listen to positive reinforcement, listen to your gut, and wear your thickest skin. It's not an easy road and rejections are numerous. But the resulting successes can be glorious."*

*"I always tell acting students that if there is anything else they enjoy they should pursue it. If you can't imagine doing anything else, then you should follow your dream with an understanding that rejection is not of you as a person. The hardest part is to keep an open heart and yet not get hurt. Remember the business in show business."*

*"Pursuit of a career in theatre is tough. One must be willing to work hard, endure disappointments, and continue to grow as a person and artist. The business is not a fair one, so one needs to have business skills and good relationships (working and otherwise), and be flexible. Have strong goals and a willingness to reassess. Go after what you want."*

*"It's a real hard business. You must have total passion and total focus on your goal. If you're one of the lucky 2 percent who works, it's still hard constantly finding work. But to get paid, raise a family, pay your bills, and buy a house doing what you love is the best feeling in the world."*

*"So much is out of our hands as performers. You have to have the drive and the desire. You have to believe that you can do it no matter what. Because people try to tear you down and tell you 'you can't because …' Don't do it for the $, because there is none. Good luck … I mean 'break a leg.'"*

*"No matter how much formal training or experience one has, it is a fact that only 2 to 3 percent of the union works [at any given time]. And the casting process remains inexplicable. Track records and training don't guarantee a job. Luck remains high on the list of who is working or not, unfortunately. Plus, since virtually everyone who auditions is skilled, most of how you get cast is on looks."*

# SECTION TWO:
# Exploring Myth and Reality

**Still with me?** I thought it was important to start out with some dissuasion from musical theatre pros to weed out any fence sitters. Performing in musical theatre and making a living at it are two totally different things. The performance aspect can be glorious, euphoric, and fantastic, while the reality of making a living in musical theatre is something else entirely. Attempting to piece together enough work to make a career in the business can be very trying and discouraging. A decision to pursue this career is not something to be taken lightly, and arming yourself with as much information as possible will help you determine the right path.

Now it's time to answer some questions. The following are FAQs regarding career choice I have heard during my time as a teacher, along with answers to the survey I gave to the seventy-five working professional actors during my sabbatical year in New York City.

## THE "T" WORD AND THE "P" WORD: "DO I HAVE THE TALENT?" VERSUS "DO I HAVE THE PASSION IT TAKES?"

Talent is an important component to possess and you won't find untalented people working professionally in theatre. But talent alone is not enough. This is where the "P" word comes into play. You must have complete passion for the art.

The following is a series of responses taken directly from the survey given to the working actors.

Rate each of the following qualities on a scale of 1 to 5 (5 being the highest) that you believe to be crucial in getting a job on Broadway and continuing to work on Broadway.

| | |
|---|---|
| Confidence | 4.8 |
| Desire/Passion | 4.75 |
| Persistence | 4.7 |
| Connections | 4.0 |
| Talent | 3.8 |
| Education | 3.5 |

I think the numbers on this list support my point and help put the talent-versus-passion question into perspective while citing other necessary qualities crucial to success in the profession. The most telling response here is that talent ended up second to last on the list of critical qualities. This was reiterated time and again in the survey, with people commenting that talent is often secondary to getting work. But although education and talent are rated the lowest, they are still thought of as important. The following are additional responses to the prompt:

**Other qualities:** Luck, loyalty, good teachers, gymnastics, knowing yourself, knowing what makes you special and different, professionalism, the ability to observe and learn from others, business sense, spiritual life, character type, prayer, being kind and patient, attitude (as in, don't give any), and looks/body type. (Four people made mention of looks. One said, *"Hate to be cynical, but a less talented pretty person often gets hired over pure talent."*)

> *"I think the most important qualities one can have are good teachers, **passion**, and discipline. Without a good leader/instructor, one can be misguided. Without **passion**, one can be dissuaded and discouraged. Without discipline, one cannot grow or continue to be competitive. It also helps to have wealthy parents. Seriously."*

> *"It's not the easiest life but can be a very freeing and fulfilling one. If you have the **passion** and desire, don't let anyone tell you not to try for it."*

> *"You must have a **passion** for the business and a strong will to keep going in the face of much rejection. You will do a lot of work for not a lot of jobs. Auditioning is part of your life, and finding a way to enjoy it will be your best gift to yourself. Every audition is your own mini play and your chance to show the directors and producers that you are the one they want for the part. They want to like you. Show them they should."*

## The Passion Path

While we are here, let's delve a little more into the important aspect of passion.

Do you remember the moment you decided you wanted to pursue your dream? This question may sound clichéd, but it is of the utmost importance. Your dreams are crucial to what you do with your life. Making a living doing the thing that gives you fulfillment is elusive. So many people are not able to do so.

I remember very clearly my moment. I was raised in a musical home where my father was a high school choir director and my mother was the organist at our church and also taught piano lessons in our house. I was always interested in the many concerts I attended, from the ones my father directed at the high school to the fantastic concerts of the Wisconsin Honors All-State ensembles (my father was one of the educators who helped create the Wisconsin Honors Project in the 1960s). However, I was always most interested in the annual musical that he directed in the fall each year. I felt so lucky to go to the high school and "hang out" while the big kids rehearsed the show. There was always a buzz in our household when the show was about to open because my parents annually entertained family and friends on the show's closing night. All aspects of this were exciting to me, but the thing I remember the most was how I was moved by the music and stories of the shows. *How to Succeed...*, *Li'l Abner*, *South Pacific* (in which I played the role of Jerome), and *The Boyfriend* were the last four shows my dad directed before leaving that job.

Being the children of musicians, my two brothers and I learned how to sing and play instruments. I played the trombone in band and sang in chorus at school. I participated in shows at my high school and loved being involved even though I never played a lead. Also, during this time our family attended performances of local musical theatre productions—both union and nonunion—as well as The Kids From Wisconsin shows at the county fairgrounds in my hometown of Waukesha. The "Kids" was a semiprofessional, high-energy show troupe of high school kids from schools around the state. It consisted of a modified big band of thirteen with twenty singers and dancers. My dad had been involved as an assistant director in the inaugural year of the Kids in 1969 and was always interested in its development. The group was a pretty big deal in Wisconsin and was the closing act for many county fairs.

The June after I graduated from high school, I was working at the very same fairgrounds, tending the tents, picking up trash, assisting lost children, earning money toward college. I made sure I was off for the Kids performance as I didn't want to miss it. As I sat and watched this particular performance, in my very private way I was incredibly moved by the emotion and energy of the performers. I had an epiphany right then and there that I remember to this day, where I realized I wanted to try to be a part of that ensemble (if I wasn't too old already) for the next summer. Afterward, when my dad went backstage to congratulate and catch up with the director and choreographer, I tagged along. Although I was intimidated by the staff and was incredibly shy (at the time), I did find out I had a year of eligibility remaining! When I shared my desire with my folks, I clearly remember my mother saying, "Oh David, do you really think you have the courage to perform with all that animation and charisma? Those kids have been doing that all their lives." Although in hindsight I realize that my mother was just trying to protect me from rejection, her words really angered and motivated me!

One year later, on the closing Sunday of the Waukesha County Fair, I stepped onstage as a singing and dancing member of The Kids From Wisconsin, and my career as a professional had begun!

What was your passion moment? Trust this moment (or moments), because it probably wasn't clouded by grade point averages, the pressure of deciding what schools you should apply to, or pleasing all of the people who think they know best. When you feel confused about your path, revisit your passion moment and see if it gives you clarity!

# IS MUSICAL THEATRE A VIABLE CAREER OPTION?

The short answer is Yes, but in blunt terms, it's an extremely difficult option. The following is information that most high school students would not think about as they delve into musical theatre but about which it is important to have some knowledge. Making a career of musical theatre means not just "doing shows" but also making a life with the earnings you receive from working. To do this, it is essential to eventually earn your Equity card and become a member of the Actors' Equity Association (AEA) union. This status not only ensures higher salaries than nonunion work (union theatres offer salaries that vary according to the type of contract they operate under) but also provides benefits such as health insurance, Social Security, and workplace safeguards.

Another perk of being a member of AEA is that it provides access to other related unions. Many actors supplement their theatre work by doing commercial, television, and film work. AFTRA (American Federation of Television and Radio Artists) and SAG (Screen Actors Guild) are sister unions of AEA. If you become a member of AEA and are in good standing for one year, you may join these unions as well.

You will hear many arguments about whether and when you should decide to become union. Once you join the union, you are not allowed to do nonunion theatre in the United States. Therefore, it is essential to have a plan regarding this important decision. Sometimes you have no choice, because union opportunities may not come your way for a long time. A lot can be said for nonunion jobs and gaining experience while you work. There is a trend now for nonunion tours and, although many union members have justifiably powerful issues against those tours, they are a way for a nonunion actor to earn good money and gain valuable experience. Also, waiting to get your card can often be the right move as you mature in the specific look or type that will be optimal for union work. Lastly, getting your card too early can have a detrimental effect on your future. Sometimes people get their cards before their skills are honed or before they are fully marketable and then find themselves floundering and not allowed to do nonunion work.

Ultimately, to make a lifelong career in musical theatre, being a member of AEA is a must.

Almost all cities with a population over 100,000 have one or more theatres that are union. In general, the larger the city, the more union theatres it has—but also the more actors with whom you will compete for jobs. Why is this important? It means you can find work in theatre in pretty much any significant-size city; your prospects don't have to be limited to Chicago, New York City, or Los Angeles.

*Is there an advantage to the three big cities?* Absolutely; there is more opportunity. *Is one city best for musical theatre?* Yes. New York City. *Why?* It not only has the most opportunity in the number of jobs available but it also is a place where regional theatres from around the country hold auditions. If you live in NYC, you could very well end up working in Akron, Ohio. But always remember: While the number of jobs is high in NYC, there is an equal amount of competition.

The following excerpt from the survey relates to career viability by asking about the annual income of the actors:

What has been your average annual income from the arts since you began your career committed solely to the performing arts? (This survey was taken in 2003-2004. A ballpark formula to calculate earnings is 2% growth a year. So, in the year 2011-2012, factor about a 16% to 17% increase in earnings.)

| Male | | Female | |
|---|---|---|---|
| $0–$10K | 2 (5%) | $0–$10K | 1 (3%) |
| $10K–$25K | 11 (29%) | $10K–$25K | 11 (33%) |
| $25K–$50K | 16 (42%) | $25K–$50K | 10 (30%) |
| $50K–$75K | 6 (16%) | $50K–$75K | 9 (27%) |
| $75K–$100K | 3 (8%) | $75K–$100K | 2 (6%) |
| $100K+ | 0 | $100K+ | 0 |
| NR (no response) | 3 | NR | 1 |

Although three-fourths of the actors are making $50,000 or less, to earn $40,000 or $50,000 a year in the business is excellent. Twenty-five percent of the men and 33 percent of the women reported averaging between $50,000 and $100,000, which is really fantastic. However, this response came from among the 2 percent of actors—mostly union—who were working at the time. The other 98 percent were being forced to find other means by which to earn a living. Also, remember that these figures are an average of their earnings during their time in the business. You can bet on inconsistency. If you expect big money you're making a big mistake! It's about the passion, right?

On the other hand, don't forget about the 2 percent of the 2 percent who make it big. They make great money and become stars. Somebody has to be in that 2 percent!

## MUST I KNOW RIGHT NOW WHETHER OR NOT I WANT TO MAKE MUSICAL THEATRE MY CAREER?

The short answer is No, but the earlier you start working toward it, the better off you will be. I didn't even consider musical theatre as a career option until the summer after my last year in college. Up to that point, I had worked four straight summer musical theatre jobs with the sole intent of earning money for my education, but I had always planned to go into teaching as a career.

However, the vast majority of the people I surveyed were devoted to the business within a year or two after college and the majority of those came out of programs directly related to the business.

The following is another component of the survey that can help answer this question even more convincingly: The median age of the men and women interviewed was 33 and 35 respectively with a composite median age of 34. The median age is significant in that, for the most part, the business is a relatively young person's business. A point could be argued that the specific casts that were interviewed skew the results. However, my sense is that they were all middle-of-the-road productions, leaning neither to the young nor the old side. **The majority of the work is for young actors, and the older you get, the fewer roles there are to be had.** If you choose to wait, you may miss out on opportunity.

On the other hand, waiting a few years isn't necessarily the worst thing to do, because with waiting come maturity and growth. Also, there is the old but true cliché "it's never too late," and people enter the business at all ages and have success. My final word on this is that if you are inclined toward this now, don't wait. Go for it!

## SHOULD I HAVE A COLLEGE EDUCATION IN ORDER TO PURSUE MUSICAL THEATRE AS A CAREER?

The short answer is Yes but the survey indicates that a small percentage of working actors (5 percent) moved directly from high school to a successful career in musical theatre. A slightly larger yet still small group (20 percent) began but did not finish a college degree and then moved directly into the business.

But the majority of people working in the business (75 percent) had at least a bachelor's or associate degree.

Of the many reasons for having a college education, life experience seems to be very high on the list:

*"Time to mature and stretch ..."*

*"... concentrated portion of your life dedicated to the task of growth ..."*

*"I grew up as a person; I found out what I did NOT want to do.*
*College is good for life and opportunity no matter what."*

*"My college life is a huge part of my confidence and who I am ..."*

*"Life experience as well as discipline, education, competition ..."*

One last piece of survey information is enlightening: 12 percent of the men and 15 percent of the women have an advanced degree or studied toward one.

## DO I HAVE TO MAJOR IN MUSICAL THEATRE
## IN ORDER TO PURSUE IT AS A CAREER?

The short answer is No, but if the pursuit of musical theatre is something you already know you want to do, working in a program devoted to it is highly advantageous.

I will once again refer to my experience because it seems especially relevant for this question. I majored in music education and received a degree in which I was certified in both choral and instrumental education. I performed in and trained for musical theatre while simultaneously working toward my degree. My music education degree gave me a lot of confidence as a singer and musician. It became obvious to me, however, that I needed to develop more thoroughly my skills in the other two realms required in musical theatre: acting and dance. After finishing my bachelor's degree at the University of Wisconsin–Madison, I moved to Chicago, where I enrolled carte blanche (a type of enrollment that enabled me to take as many classes as I wanted) at Gus Giordano Dance Center in Evanston (now Gus Giordano Dance School in Chicago), and I took acting classes at Act One in Chicago.

Although I didn't major specifically in musical theatre, my degree falls under the category of **closely related**. I took acting and dance classes that counted toward my general degree requirements, performed in university theatre productions as well as in college and summer touring groups, and worked as a performer in a theme park, all while pursuing my bachelor's degree. Lastly, I had the unique skill of gymnastics, developed in high school, which served me in many ways such as giving me highly developed coordination, a sense of body in space, and the ability to do tricks on command.

I have two close friends in the musical theatre business who also did not major in musical theatre. Their degrees were in graphic design and psychology, both falling under the category of **unrelated to the business**. They both followed paths similar to mine: training in musical theatre skills alongside their degrees, performing in college groups and productions, and working in theme parks during the summer in order to make money and continue training. The graphic design person, Tim Schultheis (who now has a headshot photography business), was primarily a dancer and gymnast and danced in a tour of *West Side Story* around the U.S. and Europe. He finished his ten-year performance career after dancing in the Broadway revival of *Joseph and the Amazing Technicolor Dreamcoat*. The psychology major, Paul Castree, is still in the business and has many Broadway as well as regional credits to his name.

It is possible to make a career in musical theatre without a degree in the field, but these two examples are more the exception than the norm. The survey reveals that of the fifty-five people who completed a degree, forty-seven (85 percent) were either in musical theatre, theatre, or closely related (vocal performance, music education, dance) programs. Of the eight non-show-business-related degrees (graphic design, speech communication, English, Italian, architecture, art history, communications, electrical engineering), it's telling to find that only one, electrical engineering, didn't have some aesthetic connection or relation to the arts.

If you did graduate, in what subject was your degree?

| Related to the business | Unrelated to the business |
|---|---|
| BFA Acting 3 | Graphic Design 1 |
| BFA Musical Theatre 13 | Speech Communication 1 |
| BA Theatre/Music 3 | English 1 |
| BA Fine Arts 1 | Electrical Engineering 1 |
| BA Theatrical Arts 3 | Italian 1 |
| BFA Drama 3 | Architecture 1 |
| BA Theatre 5 | Art History 1 |
| BA Drama 1 | Communications 1 |
| Theatre certificate 4 | |
| Musical Theatre certificate 2 | |
| BA Dance Performance 1 | |
| BM Music Ed/Voice/Therapy 1 | |
| BM Musical Theatre 1 | |
| BM Vocal Performance 4 | |
| BA Music Business 1 | |
| Bachelor of Arts 1 | |

Some other survey results support my contention that majoring in musical theatre or at least closely related programs provides great advantage:

**Do you think your training in college was vital to your success in New York and on Broadway?**

Yes  57 (76%)

No  11 (15%)

NR  2 (3%)

NA  5 (6%)

Only 15 percent of the respondents said No. The quotes that follow explain why (or why not).

**Why?**

*"Prepared me for every audition."*

*"Practical work on- and offstage."*

*"Everything you can do to raise your chances helps!"*

*"My training prepared me for auditions both with skills and confidence."*

"Helped me find an agent, and helped me greatly with auditioning."

"Good training but not enough practical application."

"Training in shows with students who were on a professional track mirrored my experience in 'Real World.'"

"Can't imagine surviving here without it!!!"

"Audition skills, discipline, self-reliance, making connections."

"I had so much to learn and it made my transition to NYC bearable. The regiment of school helped me stay focused here."

"Everyone here can sing/act/dance. I needed to have that training behind me so I could focus on the business of getting gigs!"

"Felt Brown degree gave me a certain credibility (not necessarily true but always got positive comment on it)."

"Intense training—can't do it 24/7 in NYC, have to work to pay bills, and too exhausted to take class!"

"I went to college in NYC. I learned my way around before I was 'on my own.'"

"Being well skilled in all areas of theatre/music theatre is the best way to stay versatile and consistently work in the industry."

"The better trained and versatile you are, the higher your odds are of working regularly. But it isn't a prerequisite. Being very good and persistent at one thing can get you far."

"Brought my acting up to the level of my singing."

"Audition technique and dance training."

### Why Not?

"I didn't feel college was for me; not a focused student, wanted to directly pursue the profession."

"I've found that getting to NYC and doing it is the best teacher."

"College can't possibly prepare you for the reality of the business."

"College/school did not prepare me for what I learned by watching and living among other people working in the industry."

# I WANT TO PURSUE MUSICAL THEATRE BUT ALSO THINK I SHOULD HAVE A FALLBACK DEGREE. IS THIS A GOOD IDEA?

*For students:* Let me begin this answer by stating that a college degree in any subject matter is better than no college degree at all. If you have a strong interest in a field unrelated to musical theatre, there is nothing wrong with striving for and achieving a degree in that other field. My graphic design friend, mentioned earlier, had a great interest in design and when he decided his musical theatre career was finished, he entered the graphic design field and has had great success.

I want to clarify that the above question is verbatim from students/parents. In my opinion, the answer is No, it is not a good idea. I interpret "fallback" not with any negative connotation but simply as a description of a degree that can immediately land you a job in another field. I know that I may get into trouble with parents for making this statement, but it is only my opinion. I think that if you have a degree on which to fall back, you will fall back! It is my belief that if you have no other choices regarding career, you will be more apt to work hard at the business of musical theatre. There will be no hesitation or doubt in your mind; you will pursue it with 100 percent conviction. That, in my judgment, is the only way to do it. If five years down the road you find yourself disillusioned or frustrated by the business, you can always return to school and continue your education in a field that inspires you.

*For parents:* I believe that when a student asks this question it is most likely coming from his or her parent. High school students for the most part don't think about getting a fallback degree. This question comes from the parents justifiably wanting to make sure that their child has a safety net (and I suppose, in many cases, financial situations come into play as well). This is the "practical versus passion" dilemma. Here's what I believe: When the seeds of doubt are planted, they can derail the students' path toward their passion. Essentially, if you insist that the students acquire some kind of dual or fallback degree, they will most likely not succeed in musical theatre. If they have a desire, let them try it by supporting their efforts and don't interfere. But DO insist on them earning a college degree in musical theatre. If they receive a degree in what they love, they will acquire the many skills necessary to succeed in that career plus the many life skills that come their way while in college. Even if they find that five years down the road they haven't had the success they had hoped for, they still have a college degree! This keeps the door open for continued studies in any other area they may choose. It's a win-win situation: You get the practical piece of it, and they get to pursue their passion.

## IS A BROADWAY CAREER ESSENTIAL TO SUCCESS IN MUSICAL THEATRE?

The short answer is No, but I will refer back to the "viability" question at the beginning of this section. You will find that there is union work to be had in most cities. Many people find a niche in local theatre and are cast in production after production. They lead comfortable lives and are fulfilled by the work they do. However, a possible and likely scenario is as follows: You are a petite blonde—a specific leading female ingénue type with a beautiful classical soprano singing voice. Unfortunately, in the city where you have decided to settle, there lives a woman who is your exact type and who has been doing these roles for the past three years. You are her equal in every way but she got there first. She has the advantage of having the confidence of the producers and directors of that city's union theatre, and they can count on her to produce as she is a known commodity. As talented as you are, you may not work, at least not as a lead, in this theatre community.

Broadway has a similar "small world" effect and you will often see the same people working year after year—but there is still more opportunity to be had in NYC.

*"… can't emphasize enough the training I got in regional theatre and off-Broadway."*

*"I haven't worked on Broadway but I've done national tours, musical theatre concerts all over Europe, and regional theatre at some of the top LORT (League of Resident Theatres) houses in the U.S., and I love my life. Last year I did* My Fair Lady, A Little Night Music, *an Irving Berlin concert, two productions of* Jekyll and Hyde, *and* The Fantasticks. *All lead roles and I completely support myself. There is so much work out there that is not Broadway but you have to live in NYC to really set yourself up—I would love one Broadway show to help make my LORT life even better!"*

## IF I BECOME A MUSICAL THEATRE ACTOR, WILL I HAVE TO TAKE SURVIVAL JOBS SUCH AS WAITING TABLES?

The answer to this is unknown, but the chances are likely. Very few people are able to make a living solely on Broadway and/or other stages. Many seek employment through television, film, commercial, and voice-over work. This is the most beneficial type of work because it not only pays extremely well but also can contribute in positive ways to your stage career. A casting consultant in NYC named Bob Luke says the fastest way to Broadway is through TV. You can't beat the exposure it gives you. Many NY stage actors make frequent appearances on shows filmed in NYC such as *Law and Order* to supplement their incomes. Others find the work in television and film more rewarding and leave the stage altogether. Megan Mullaly, of *Will and Grace*, was an actress in Broadway shows including the 1990s revivals of *Grease* and *How To Succeed…* and then made the rare move to TV star.

An overwhelming 92 percent of the people who filled out the survey answered that they had had at least one type of survival job (three people did not respond, three never had to work a survival job). The most common job was waiting tables, which is logical because it is the most flexible job you can have and it can pay very well. Other jobs or positions mentioned include catering waiter, temping/computer work, bartending, teaching, construction work, painting, messenger, tech/stagehand, and telemarketing.

One last way to supplement an income is through unemployment insurance. Of course this can happen only if you've already had work (at least six months in a year's period of time) and qualify for benefits. It can sustain an actor and offers the advantage of maximizing his or her opportunity to study and audition.

# SECTION THREE:
# School Selection

## NOW THAT I'VE MADE UP MY MIND TO PURSUE MUSICAL THEATRE, WHAT SHOULD I DO NEXT?

You should continue to train your primary skill (voice, acting, or dance) but also begin to develop the two other skills. For instance, if acting is your primary skill, begin to take voice lessons and dance classes. The earlier you start this process, the better. All college-level musical theatre programs have a central goal of turning out balanced performers. Being a "triple threat" increases your chance of employment.

Another helpful skill to have, even if it's at a beginner level, is piano. If you are able to play notes from a sheet of music on the piano and can teach yourself a song without having help, you are ahead of the game and will save yourself money. The higher your level of musicianship, the more marketable you become.

*"I feel these days you have to be a triple threat."*

## DO SCHOOLS ACTUALLY OFFER A DEGREE IN MUSICAL THEATRE?

Yes, many schools offer a degree in musical theatre. Musical theatre programs are a more recent phenomenon in colleges and universities. Most schools are still known for either their music or theatre programs. Now, however, excellent schools do tender this degree, and more and more schools offer some kind of training in this area.

## SCHOOL TYPE: WHAT KIND OF SCHOOL SHOULD I ATTEND?

*"I think different colleges/conservatories have different strengths and weaknesses. When choosing a school, be sure you know what it is you want out of your training. Don't be afraid to ask what the school thinks of the education it provides, and check its list of graduates—that will give you something to go by."*

Better advice couldn't be offered.

Some schools offer degrees with a very focused, laser approach with minimal "core curriculum" requirements, while others offer degrees with a wider requirement of liberal arts to give you more breadth of knowledge. A number of schools offer contract or individualized major program degrees where you and the school tailor a program to your needs. Lastly, some schools offer associate degrees, which require a two- or three-year obligation.

You need to determine for yourself what type of program is best suited for you. To make an informed decision, begin by researching the required curriculum for the school's degree and see if it fits with what you are interested in pursuing.

There are so many things to consider besides the type of degree you are after. In what part of the state or country do you wish to attend college? Does the school have the social atmosphere you desire? Is it near a big city where you can attend professional theatre? Tuition and room and board prices vary dramatically; what is your budget?

## WHAT SCHOOLS SHOULD I CONSIDER?

*"I am coming from the point of view of a B'Way dancer. I do not regret or undermine my education. But going to a conservatory with connections is absolutely a fast track to professional work. And the 'training' schools really pump out amazingly confident people who know how to audition well, a very separate skill."*

This is the most popular question that I am asked. In the past I didn't have a comprehensive list to offer and never had enough time to research the possibilities. While on sabbatical leave I came across a special edition of the publication *Back Stage* that had a listing of all theatre programs in the U.S. I took this listing, researched to see which schools offered musical theatre, and found that most tender either some kind of degree or at least in-depth training.

I also found several publications designed specifically for the purpose of researching theatre programs. What follows is a list of the publications available, some with the published product descriptions.

---

### *Directory of Theatre Training Programs* by Peg Lyons & P.J. Tumielwicz

"Any prospective student of theatre will find this unique guidebook totally indispensable. It is filled with valuable information on programs in small liberal arts colleges and large universities as well as specialized conservatories."     —*American Reference Books Annual*

"Profiles admissions, tuition, faculty, theatre training, curriculum, facilities, productions, and philosophy of training at 475 programs around the country and abroad: drama schools, colleges, universities, conservatories, and undergraduate and graduate degrees. Arranged by state and then alphabetically by the name of the school, this directory lists detailed information about theatre programs: name of department head, address, telephone number, fax, URL, cost, number of students, degrees offered, admission and financial information, number of faculty and their degrees, facilities and productions, and a brief description. An index with the alphabetical listing of schools is included."

—Publisher's product description

### College Guide for Performing Arts Majors: The Real-World Admission Guide for Dance, Music, and Theater Majors (Performing Arts Major's College Guide) by Carole Everett

This is the standard publication that you will find in most high school guidance counseling offices. Definitely a valuable tool. —DL

### A Guide to College Choices for the Performing and Visual Arts
by Ed Schoenberg and Kavin Buck

"The performing and visual arts niche to college admissions is a specialty that few students and college counselors know how to navigate. This guidebook simplifies the process, makes it less daunting, and is very straightforward. It offers practical, insightful information and helpful hints to assist students in their pursuit of an education in the performing and visual arts. *A Guide to College Choices for the Performing Visual Arts* is a must read for any student interested in studying the performing and visual arts in college." —Publisher's product description

### Creative Colleges: A Guide for Student Actors, Artists, Dancers, Musicians and Writers by Elaina Loveland

"Written exclusively for college-bound students interested in the creative arts, this updated guide addresses the unique concerns of students pursuing an education in acting, art, dance, music, and writing. Everything students need to know about deciding which type of program is the best fit for them is included—from taking standardized tests and filing for financial aid to focusing on specific needs such as preparing for auditions and creating artistic portfolios. More than 200 art, drama, dance, music, and creative writing programs in arts conservatories, liberal arts colleges, and universities are profiled with critical information such as degrees and concentrations offered, faculty information, cost of attendance, scholarship availability, and alumni accomplishments. Also included are day-in-the-life snapshots of students, frequently asked questions, sample admission essays, and tips from faculty." —Publisher's product description

### Passion For The Arts: College Admissions Handbook—Visual and Performing Arts College Information created by Highland Park High School, Highland Park, Illinois, and updated by New Trier High School, Winnetka, Illinois

This is a good starter resource and will help students and parents get their feet wet as they begin the process of selecting programs and schools. The resource is a PDF file on the New Trier High School website, **newtrier.k12.il.us**.

Once at the website, click on Performing Arts, then click on Passion For The Arts–Informational Materials. —DL

## *schoolsfortheatre.com*

This highly useful resource lets you cut straight to the chase. The website allows you to narrow your search by region or major type. When you do a search, a list of schools will come up and from there you can explore the different degrees the school offers and find general information as well. Some schools provide audition information, the curriculum and season of shows, a list of faculty and alumni, and a link to the school's own website. It's very up to date. —DL

I can't stress enough the importance of picking the school that is right for you. It doesn't serve you to end up in a high-profile school if you work best in a more intimate setting that has less pressure. However, some of the top schools, such as Carnegie Mellon University (CMU), University of Michigan, University of Cincinnati College Conservatory of Music (CCM), and New York University (NYU), to name a few, will offer more opportunity if you are in good standing. Students will have the chance to perform in showcases for talent agencies from both NY and LA. To be seen by a host of talent agencies is a tremendous advantage when you are about to embark for one of these cities, and it is an exceptional advantage if you can procure an agent right away.

The following is extracted directly from the Cincinnati CCM's website:

## MUSICAL THEATRE

Musical Theatre today is an impressive art form. Capacity audiences worldwide attest to the popularity of musicals created on the stages of Broadway and the West End. It is the most collaborative of all the arts, bringing together the composer, lyricist, playwright, choreographer, conductor, designer, and performer in a unique way. Today a performer must be able to sing and dance and act with technical mastery and craft. And that is the minimum requirement!

The College–Conservatory of Music (CCM) provides professional conservatory training designed to help students become mature and polished performers. With its emphasis on imagination, analysis, and technical skill, our program provides the craft to master a popular art form: capturing in sound and movement those universal emotions that have made the musical America's most visible contribution to world theatre. At CCM we are in the business of turning out "triple threats"—talented young people who can sing, dance, and act with equal accomplishment. Our graduates can think and do, can explore their art in depth, and can communicate in fluid and expressive ways. We have a demanding and difficult course of training with intensive course work and little time for relaxation. Discipline and professionalism are essential components of this program and provide our graduates with the wherewithal to survive in a highly competitive field.

Our classes are small so that each student can receive a great deal of attention from the faculty. **We are committed to helping students find employment in an overcrowded profession by providing master classes with professionals in the field and BY SHOWCASING OUR SENIOR CLASS IN NEW YORK CITY.** Our graduates are working on Broadway, in regional theatres, on national tours, and abroad. In addition to performing, alumni succeed in related areas as musical directors, choreographers, writers, agents, or casting directors. The skills acquired in our classes provide an excellent background for whatever artistic endeavors our graduates wish to pursue. The network of CCM professionals often helps our students make the difficult transition to a career in the arts.

*Why is a showcase opportunity so critical?* Just as getting good grades was important when you were a freshman in high school because of its influence on your future college placement (whether you realized it then or not), having the opportunity to secure a talent agent directly out of college can influence the kind of track you find yourself on as a professional. A talent agent will send you to "agent call" auditions for lead roles. This is the "lead role" track. Without an agent, you are reduced to attending chorus calls (the "chorus role" track) or EPAs (Equity principal auditions), which are less likely to offer opportunity to advance to a lead role in a major show (although it's not impossible).

*Is getting a talent agent through a college showcase the only way to acquire one?* No, there are several ways: persistent mailings of your information (headshot, resume, cover letter) to agencies, having agents and/or scouts see you in a show or showcase, and being introduced through a friend. However, to have agents see you as you are finishing your degree and take you on at that point is a tremendous advantage. There's always the occasion where you may end up with an agent who is wrong for you, but in general having a good agent is paramount to ultimate success in musical theatre.

## School Visits/Application/Preparation/Auditions

When you have determined what type of degree you are interested in pursuing, it's time to visit and then apply to the schools that offer the education you desire.

Visits to schools are essential and will often sway you one way or another when making decisions regarding the schools to which you apply. Be sure to have a list of important items to look at, such as facilities, dormitories (and their proximity), and the city close by. Ask about the education the school offers and what projects its graduates are doing. Remember, you are interviewing the school.

With the help of your guidance counselor, you'll complete applications to a number of schools. Each school will have specific admission requirements and its own deadlines for application and audition scheduling. This information can be found in a number of ways: websites, brochures, your high school guidance counseling office, or one of the publications listed earlier in this section. The number of schools to which you apply is up to you.

At the same time you should be preparing to audition for these programs. Each school will have specific requirements for its auditions. You'll probably find and work up two or three songs and a couple of monologues that will suffice for most of the auditions. Work with your voice teacher, vocal coach, and monologue coach to make sure you are on track. Give yourself the opportunity to "perform" your auditions for an audience. This is very important because it will help you deal effectively with nerves.

For detailed preparation information, consider the book *I Got In!* by Mary Anna Dennard. Subtitled "The Ultimate College Audition Guide for Acting and Musical Theatre," it is a highly useful tool to help you prepare auditions for college programs. The author goes into detail about audition components and how to choose and prepare songs and monologues, speaks to the different types of auditions you may encounter, and lists valuable quotes from professors at high-profile schools. It's definitely worth having this book at the beginning of your organizational process.

# SECTION FOUR:
# Down the Road

Although it may seem a bit premature to talk about what to expect as you finish your degree, it pays to consider this prior to your entry into a program that trains you for such a difficult profession. The following comments are perhaps similar to "A Preposterous Idea" in that they share some of the realities of the business. Additionally, more results from the survey may be useful as you contemplate a career in musical theatre.

## Training/Study

You'll remain "a student for life," according to the consensus of the survey respondents:

> *"It (college) is a good basis … but you still take classes and study once you get here."*

> *"I feel it's vital to study your craft—always taking voice and acting lessons."*

Perhaps one of the most important pieces of information compiled from the survey is that 95 percent of all the actors continue to study. This means that, although the college degree is important, it is only the beginning of a life of constant refreshment and training. Maintaining your primary skill and continuous training of other skills as well as keeping your body in shape with a gym membership are definite musts in today's musical theatre world. The disciplines mentioned in the survey—voice, acting, dance, gym, yoga, and Pilates–include nothing new.

When Idina Menzel won the 2004 Tony award for Best Performance by a Lead Actress in a Musical for her role in *Wicked*, included in those she thanked was her voice teacher.

The pros I interviewed mentioned the importance of continued training:

> *"Once you finish school, it is not over. Classes are the key to being a successful working actor. After auditions, send a follow-up thank-you to the casting directors (especially if you have been called back). It keeps you fresh in their minds and you have a better chance of their remembering who you are next time. Also, be kind to EVERYONE you work with. You never know if they are going to be casting, directing, or choreographing the next Broadway show."*

> *"I feel that you can never stop training. It keeps you healthy—in the loop and inspired."*

## Finances

Financial information should also be considered. Upon completion of your college degree, if you haven't already, you'll need to decide in what city you'd like to live and work. Any kind of move and settlement is expensive, but moving to a major city is dramatically so. At the point in time when you need a lot of seed money, graduating college students are historically at their poorest! Check out the following survey answers:

**How much money did you bring or start out with as an independent in NYC?**

| Male | | Female | |
|---|---|---|---|
| $0–$500 | 5 (14%) | $0–$500 | 7 (23%) |
| $501–$1,000 | 11 (29%) | $501–$1,000 | 4 (13%) |
| $1,000–$2,000 | 6 (16%) | $1,000–$2,000 | 10 (32%) |
| $2,001–$5,000 | 8 (21%) | $2,001–$5,000 | 4 (13%) |
| $5,000+ | 8 (21%) | $5,000+ | 6 (16%) |
| NR | 3 | NR or N/A | 3 |

Most of those who fall in the $0–$500 range either were older (and came years ago when the cost of living was much lower) or had financial help. The Peggy Sawyer story (in *42nd Street*, where she shows up in NY with only a pair of tap shoes and lands the lead in a Broadway show) is a rarity. Although these numbers are from 2004, the information is still useful. If you add a 2 percent per year increase to the figures above and below, you will be able to predict each scenario quite closely.

You can minimize your initial expenses when moving to NYC (or any other city) by either living with friends or subletting. This eliminates the need to pay first and last month's rent, a security deposit, and all of the start-up costs for cable, gas, electricity, etc. I suppose it's possible, under the right circumstances (staying with friends, sublet), to move with $1,000, but this just gets you there and settled. A job would be necessary almost immediately.

Even with an inexpensive living situation, many start-up or getting-situated expenses are necessary: headshots ($400-$750), capacity to print your resume (perhaps you'll come with a computer and printer that will suffice), and mailings to agencies if you don't already have one (envelopes, paper, stamps: at least $100 a year).

A better scenario is a sublet and $2,500. This buys you perhaps two months of time before needing to find a survival job. If you insist on your own rental, you'll probably need $4,000–$5,000 to get settled and to buy two months of time before a survival job is necessary.

# HEADSHOTS

While we're on the topic, here are a few things to keep in mind regarding headshots. You can spend anywhere from $25 to $1,600! Yes, with a good digital camera you can probably have a friend take some headshots of you, and you could get away with spending only $25 or so to reproduce them. My suggestion is, if you are serious about your career you should work with a professional photographer who specializes in headshots for musical theatre. As tempting or convenient as it may be, do not go to your local portrait photographer, as most are unaware of the style of shot being done in this business.

If you are planning to move to New York or Los Angeles, go to **reproductions.com** and search through its index of photographers until you find portraits that resonate with you. (For Chicago, go to **actingstudiochicago.com** and find the Headshot Photographers page.) Contact that photographer and spend some time getting to know him or her. Sit down for fifteen or twenty minutes and ask questions. The photographer needs to take an interest in you as well so that he or she can make you feel comfortable and photograph you in your best light. This relationship is incredibly important!

You shouldn't need more than a couple of changes of clothing. If you are constantly changing into a different look, you aren't spending enough time connecting with the photographer. Avoid trendy clothing, as you will want to get at least a few years out of your headshots. Your goal is to achieve the most natural look possible. No makeup for men. Women, in addition to paying for a photographer, you will want a makeup artist at your shoot. Do your own makeup and hair and then have the makeup artist tweak it a little. Avoid having the makeup artist do a falsely glamorous impression of you because you need to look like your picture! (If your headshot lands you an interview or audition and you arrive not looking like your picture, this will clearly work against you.) A high-quality headshot in New York will cost anywhere from $400 to $750.

You can spend more than that, but be prudent in your choice. If you find a photographer whose portraits resonate with you, you don't need to spend more on a well-known name.

Did you have any financial help?

| Male | Female |
|------|--------|
| Yes 18 (44%) | Yes 10 (33%) |
| No 23 (56%) | No 20 (66%) |
| | NA 1 |

It is a significant plus if you have financial help to start. It's important, however, to establish yourself financially in a short period of time in order to create an atmosphere of self-reliance. Doing so gives you confidence and a sense of accomplishment—both requirements for success in this business.

Although the time may be a long way off, financial planning for starting your career and continued training have to be taken into account.

## Ethnicity

Caucasian  54 (89%)
Puerto Rican  1 (1.6%)
African-American  4 (6.6%)
Asian-American  2 (3.3%)
NR  14

Unfortunately, there are no surprises here. All union production companies and theatres are committed by Equity rules to nontraditional casting (see page 26). I was aware that for my production of *Footloose* (at Westchester Broadway Theatre) only one African-American actor auditioned. It seems a contributing factor is the reluctance of actors of ethnic descent to pursue jobs that they don't see themselves in traditionally. If I'd had the opportunity to interview the casts of shows that have a predominance of ethnic actors, the numbers would obviously be dramatically different. However, on the whole, I would say that the percentages listed are perhaps skewed a little to the extreme but quite close to reality.

Since my time in New York City in 2003-'04, a subtle evolution has continued in this area in the theatre. The Non-Traditional Casting Project was founded in 1986 to examine problems of racism—and other kinds of discrimination—in theatre, film, and television. (To learn more about the project, visit the website of the National Endowment for the Arts, **arts.gov/resources/Accessibility/NTCP.html**, to read "The Non-Traditional Casting Project" by Sharon Jensen.)

High-profile nontraditional casting was evident in the 1990s when actors such as Lea Salonga (a woman of Asian descent who played the role of Eponine in *Les Miserables* on Broadway) and Audra McDonald (an African-American woman who played the role of Carrie in the revival of *Carousel*, also on Broadway) were cast in traditionally Caucasian roles. Seemingly trendsetting at the time, this is a more common practice now. Additionally, more producers, composers, and writers are creating and supporting shows with ethnic actors and plot lines. An ever-increasing amount of productions on Broadway accurately reflect the ethnic diversity of America. Shows such as *In the Heights* and *Memphis* have seen great success in the past few years and attract an equally diverse audience. Although neither dramatic nor as quick as some would like, a positive advancement continues in nontraditional casting since the Non-Traditional Casting Project was founded.

---

## Here are the Equity rules on Nontraditional Casting.

### 23. DISCRIMINATION (See also Rule 43 Non-Traditional Casting)

(A) The parties hereto affirm their commitment to the policy that employment hereunder shall be without discrimination on the basis of sex, race, color, creed, national origin, age, disability, sexual orientation, or political persuasion or belief. Consistent with the foregoing and with the procedure set forth in Rule 5(E)(4), it is the intention of the parties that the casting of productions will be conducted in a manner which provides equal and fair consideration to all Actors including, but not limited to: Actors with disabilities, ethnic minorities, seniors and women.

### 43. NON-TRADITIONAL CASTING (See also Rule 23 Discrimination)

The parties recognize the principle of Non-traditional Casting. The parties further agree, the foregoing notwithstanding, that there can be no interference with the contractual rights or artistic discretion of the playwright, director, or choreographer. Subject to these limitations, the Producer will attempt to achieve Non-traditional Casting.

(A) Non-traditional Casting is defined as the casting of Actors with disabilities, ethnic minorities (African-American, Asian-American, Hispanic-American, Native-American), seniors and women in roles where race, gender, age or the presence or absence of a disability is not germane.

(B) Quarterly meetings will be held between Equity and the League to assure that this Non-traditional Casting policy is being observed and to monitor its implementation.

(C) An analysis of all productions in performance during the previous quarter shall be conducted at these quarterly meetings.

(D) If a dispute under this rule cannot be resolved by the parties at the quarterly meeting, the dispute shall be submitted to grievance and arbitration in accordance with Rule 4.

## Connections

Connections were mentioned earlier, in the section pertaining to qualities the actors believed to be crucial in getting a job. Being connected is something you achieve through working hard, by cultivating good relationships, and by returning time and again to audition for a show or director, etc. This "quality" cannot be underestimated. In the twelve months of my sabbatical, I was offered five separate projects, and three of them had some kind of connection involved. Two of those five never required me to audition. If I look back at my musical theatre career before I started teaching, most of the jobs I got were through some kind of connection that I had nurtured.

*"Unfortunately, after many years in the business, I think that it is apparent that talent plays such a minor role in casting and booking work. Foremost, I believe that persistence, desire, knowing the right people, [and] being in the right place at the right time are truly the factors that lead to a majority of casting. Talent is very often a factor that is considered last if not least."*

*"It's all about who you know."*

*"Connections include networking through employment, classes, seminars, and especially auditions. But most important, playing well with others."*

*"[Connections] can mean a lot if they know your work. ... I've been asked to do shows without having to audition."*

## Advice from the Pros

Final quotes and thoughts from professionals.

*"Be prepared. Learn the business. See everything you can, good and bad. Off-Broadway is as important as Broadway. The economics are much tougher and the pay is half of what Broadway is, but it is some of the best work creatively being done in NY."*

*"I feel it's so important to always be working to be better at anything one chooses. 'Keep those dreams alive!' Doing showcases, taking classes taught by casting directors if they don't know you. No role is too small and you must want it more than anything!!!"*

*"Life experience influences your work (acting, etc.) more than just study. Be careful not to get pulled into associating only with fellow actors and theatre folks— you become too one-dimensional. Make sure you make time to have a life—believe it or not, it makes you a much more interesting performer than the person who eats, lives, and breathes only theatre (that person is a boring typical actor). You want to be the interesting person with other fascinating hobbies and interests."*

*"1. There is a time and season for everything. 2. God and family come first before everything—I think they should. 3. Never give up on your dreams!"*

*"Seems that if you're tremendously proficient in voice or dance, the other doesn't matter. If you're not a "dance 10" or "sing 10," it becomes more important to have both skills. I have rarely found acting ability to make or break getting a job."*

*"Didn't know much about the business end of the 'business'—it's very important—half of getting a job. Need to know how to write good cover letters, thank-yous, follow-up cards to casting people after auditions, etc. Having a good reputation helps—everyone talks. Small community. Casting wants people who are easy to work with, are friendly with others, and don't create problems. Connections help to get your face out there!"*

## Step into the Spotlight

I've tried to show that choosing musical theatre as a career can be a daunting proposition. The important things to remember are:

- Earning a college degree is essential (even if it's not in musical theatre) because college offers an atmosphere that nurtures growth and maturity and provides the opportunity for you to become a more well-rounded individual.

- You should find the type of school that not only will train you well but also will give you confidence as you enter the profession.

- Know before delving into college and the career afterward that you'll always need to continue training.

- The inconsistency of employment is something you can count on; it means you'll need to rely on your passion for the art (and be humble enough to take a survival job) to see you through the downtimes.

The fact that you're considering musical theatre as a career already indicates you have a love for the art form. Never lose sight of this important quality and don't hesitate to revisit your *passion path*. Musical theatre can be a glorious career and provide deep fulfillment. If you always keep that thought front and center, you'll stay on a successful course.

# part two

## THE MUSICAL THEATRE CAREER AND NEW YORK CITY

*Information and Reflections on the Pursuit of a Broadway Show*

# SECTION ONE:
# When You Get There

## Survival Information for NYC

**"New York, New York, it's a helluva town!"** Leonard Bernstein's song from *On the Town* (lyrics by Betty Comden and Adolph Green) about the great city in the 1940s still holds true today. New York City IS a glamorous place, but there is also a flip side. When you *visit* the city as a theatre-goer or tourist, and perhaps some of you have, your experience is quite different from when you live there. As a theatre-goer, you might stay in a hotel in Times Square, eat in restaurants within walking distance, walk down the Disney-influenced Forty-second Street, and take in incredible Broadway plays and musicals. You might catch a glimpse of a star or see the premiere of a new show. There is a wonderful buzz in the theatre district and you feel as though you are at the center of the world.

When you *live* in New York City, you ride the subway and, most probably, live in a distant neighborhood. You go to the local grocery store, eat in local restaurants (if you can afford it), and are very rarely in Times Square. You become familiar with which day is garbage collection day (the garbage bags go right on the sidewalk in front of every dwelling) and take notice of the healthy rat population (don't worry, they mind their own business). You wait on subway platforms that are usually about twenty-five degrees warmer than the street above (nice in the winter, pretty disgusting in the summer). And, you are first repulsed by, but ultimately get used to, the smell.

That's not to say it isn't really exciting to live in New York! It truly is, and when you move there and begin pursuing your passion by going to auditions and taking class, the city becomes even more impressive as you discover all it has to offer. So, these are the questions I thought were relevant and important for helping you begin your transition from dreams to reality.

## Living Situation

Where was the first place you lived and/or stayed in NYC?

| Male | | Female | |
|---|---|---|---|
| With Friend(s) | 10 (24%) | With Friend(s) | 6 (18%) |
| Family | 5 (12%) | Family | 2 (6%) |
| Sublet | 14 (34%) | Sublet | 6 (16%) |
| Rental | 11 (27%) | Rental | 18 (53%) |
| YMCA | 1 (2%) | Dorm | 2 (6%) |

If you were in a Sublet or Rental, did you have roommates?

| Male | | Female | |
|---|---|---|---|
| Yes | 20 (77% of 26) | Yes | 19 (79% of 24) |
| No | 6 (23% of 26) | No | 3 (13% of 24) |
| | | NR | 2 |

The answers to these two questions support my prediction that you will most likely begin your time in NYC either staying with friends or in a sublet (about half of the survey respondents did one or the other) and that you will have a roommate. It just makes sense from a financial standpoint, and it also offers a support system.

What is your monthly rent?

| Male | | Female | |
|---|---|---|---|
| $0 – $1,000 | 24 (60%) | $0 – $1,000 | 13 (41%) |
| $1,001 – $1,500 | 8 (20%) (1M) | $1,001 – $1,500 | 8 (25%) (1M) |
| $1,501 – $2,000 | 7 (18%) | $1,501 – $2,000 | 7 (22%) (2M) |
| $2,001+ | 0 | $2,001+ | 4 (13%) (2M) |
| (1 NR) | | (2 NR) | |

*2004 figures. Factor a 2% increase a year to estimate rent in current-day figures.*
*(M) denotes mortgage.*

Here's another example of the astronomical rent in NYC. It's probably impossible to find a single dwelling apartment in Manhattan (studio or one-bedroom) for under $1,000. To live in Manhattan, a newcomer would best be served by having at least one roommate or perhaps two to split rent. Those paying in the $0-to-$1,000-a-month category were either living off the island or had a roommate.

I think one of the most important pieces of information that people provided, though it wasn't asked for, is the fact that some are paying mortgages (indicated above as M in parentheses). It's revealing and heartening to find that actors own property and work consistently enough to make regular payments. If I had asked about this specifically, I have a feeling I'd have had more responses than just the five who made mention of it.

Where do you reside?

| Male | | Female | | Combined | |
|---|---|---|---|---|---|
| Manhattan | 30 (73%) | Manhattan | 18 (53%) | Manhattan | 48 (64%) |
| Queens | 4 (10%) | Queens | 7 (21%) | Queens | 11 (15%) |
| New Jersey | 5 (12%) | New Jersey | 3 (9%) | New Jersey | 8 (11%) |
| Brooklyn | 1 (2%) | Brooklyn | 2 (6%) | Brooklyn | 3 (4%) |
| Other | 1 (2%) | Other | 4 (12%) | Other | 5 (6%) |
| [Yonkers] | | [Connecticut 2, Westchester 1, Pennsylvania 1] | | | |

The fact that the majority of actors live in Manhattan speaks to the success of the actors themselves. I didn't interview the struggling actor who is relegated to working survival jobs. Rent in Manhattan is incredibly expensive and, for an actor who first comes to the city without a high-paying job (production contract), it's more cost-effective to live in New Jersey, Queens, or a relatively inexpensive neighborhood of Brooklyn.

*"Very expensive in Manhattan now. Be prepared to have roommates.*
*Come with friends for support."*

## Tools

Publications or books you found useful in your early years in NYC
The following are ranked in order of importance according to the survey respondents. I've made a few comments on these publications you should consider using as reference when you move to NYC:

*Back Stage*, **mentioned in 37 survey responses.** Without question, this is the most important and useful publication you can have in the business. It is the number one source for audition information. Auditions are separated into Equity and non-Equity Stage, Union and non-Union Film, etc. It also provides about four hundred reviews of theatre productions every year and has endless information regarding classes and workshops. Occasionally it will have special sections on schools or shows and many articles pertaining to the business. I personally found that having the actual weekly paper was a plus because I could take it to auditions and I liked the tactile hard copy. If you subscribe for a year it is significantly cheaper than buying it off the newsstand. In 2005, because of online competition, *Back Stage* revamped itself, changing its tagline from "The Performing Arts Weekly" to "The Actor's Resource." It updated its website to reflect daily activity and incorporated some of the new-media casting tools that were being used by other websites. In the early '90s, *Back Stage* acquired *Ross Reports* (renamed *Call Sheet*, see below) and added that resource of up-to-date agent and casting director information to its arsenal. It still offers a weekly hardcopy magazine as well. *Back Stage* continues as a valuable resource. **backstage.com**.

**Ross Reports (now called *Call Sheet*), mentioned by 13.** This is the second-most important publication, according to the actors surveyed. It lists all talent and casting agencies on both coasts as well as all TV shows in production and where they are cast and filmed. It can be a daunting task to find an agent out of this book, so it's best to have a casting consultant help you narrow down the list of agencies to pursue. *Call Sheet Online*, which you'll find on the *Back Stage* website, may be an even more reliable source because it is as current as it can be. You can search by agent or casting director and have access to four distinct directories: New York, Los Angeles, Chicago, and Florida. You can even do an advanced search by location, talent, and entertainment field. My suggestion is to check out the subscription options listed at the website and subscribe to a combination package of *Back Stage* and *Call Sheet*. There are several options, based on hard-copy and online preferences.

**The New York Agent Book (K Callan), listed on 11 surveys.** The author is an actress in television and film who has been around the business for a long time. Her two resources—*The New York Agent Book* and *The Los Angeles Agent Book*—have valuable insights into the agent world. (She's also written several industry books to help actors, directors, and screenwriters; one is listed below.) This book is a guide to not just the agents in New York (or Los Angeles), but also to starting out in the business. It starts with a section designed to prepare you before you even leave your hometown. This is followed up with sections that help you get to know New York, become your own "agent," and increase your self-knowledge (knowing what is marketable about you), plus a section describing what agencies do. The first hundred-plus pages focus on your education and preparation. The agent section, near the end of the book, has contact data, useful background information about each agency, and the names of the agents and what they specialize in. This book is another great resource for about $20. Currently it is updated about once every four years, so the agency information can get out of date.

**Theatrical Index, listed 4 times.** To quote **ascap.com**: "Subtitled 'The Voice of the Theatre,' the weekly edition of *Theatrical Index* is filled with information on musicals, plays scheduled to open, and the current theatrical offerings. Specifically geared to professionals within the theater industry, it contains information on producers, agents and publicists." This is a very expensive publication. I'm not familiar with this publication (couldn't afford it) so I cannot recommend for or against it.

*Audition* (**Michael Shurtleff**), **mentioned 3 times.** Although it was first published in 1978, it is still the number one and most trusted publication available to help you prepare for auditions. A definite must if you have not already read it. It's readily available in paperback at a reasonable price.

*Not For Tourists*, **listed 2 times.** I was still using my *NFT* long after I'd gotten to know the city. It is a detailed, pocket-sized book of maps of Manhattan with vital information regarding transportation. A highly useful tool.

*the organized actor* (**Leslie Becker**), **mentioned 2 times**. This workbook and planning device helped me set goals and keep track of important audition information as I worked through my year of pursuing musical theatre in NYC. It is a tool that I highly recommend, especially at the beginning of a career.

Others that were mentioned:
*Acting As a Business/New Edition: Strategies for Success* (Brian O'Neil), **2**
*New York Times*, **2**
*Cheap Bastards Guide to NYC*
*How to Sell Yourself as an Actor* (K Callan)
*Time Out: the World's Living Guide* (**newyork.timeout.com**)
*Village Voice* (weekly local newspaper, **villagevoice.com**)
**Actors Equity website (actorsequity.org)**
*Theatre World* (statistical and pictorial record of the Broadway and Off-Broadway season)
*Respect for Acting* (Uta Hagen)
*On Acting* (Sanford Meisner)
*Acting Professionally: Raw Facts About Careers in Acting* (Robert Cohen)
*Callback* (Ginger Howard Friedman, **gingerauditiontraining.com**)
**Lincoln Center Library**
*Zen and the Art of Archery*
**TVI Actors Studio**

In addition to the resources listed above, theatre professional friends of mine suggest the following:
*Auditioning: An Actor-Friendly Guide* (Joanna Merlin with a foreword by Harold Prince)
*It Would Be So Nice If You Weren't Here...My Journey Through Show Business* (Charles Grodin)
*Being an Actor* (Simon Callow)

*Theater Artist's Resource: The Watson-Guptill Guide to Academic and Conservatory Programs, Studios and Studio Schools, Workshops, Festivals and Conferences, Artists' Colonies and Residencies, Internships and Apprenticeships* (Ruth Mayleas)

A final suggestion on finding the tools of the trade is to take a trip to either Samuel French or Dramatists and explore their bookstores when you are in NYC.

Samuel French Inc.
2 W. 25th St., #45, New York, NY 10010
(212) 206-8990

Dramatists Play Service Inc.
440 Park Avenue South, New York, NY 10016
(212) 683-8960

## Employment

Did you come to NYC with or without an Equity card?

| Male | Female |
|------|--------|
| With  18 (44%) | With  16 (47%) |
| Without  23 (56%) | Without  18 (53%) |

A little less than half the respondents came to New York with their Equity card. This means they got their cards either through summer stock during college, in regional theatre, or in a national tour. As you can see, it's not a necessity to have your card before arriving in NYC.

How long were you in NYC before you got your first Broadway show?

| Male | Female |
|------|--------|
| Came to NYC with show  2 (7%) | Came to NYC with show  2 (8%) |
| Less than one year  6 (21%) | Less than one year  5 (20%) |
| From one to two years  2 (7%) | From one to two years  3 (12%) |
| From two to five years  10 (36%) | From two to five years  8 (32%) |
| More than five years  8 (29%) | More than five years  7 (28%) |
| NA  13 | NA  9 |

This goes to tenacity and revisits the *passion path*. How tenacious are you? Some 65 percent of the men and 60 percent of the women waited at least two years for a Broadway show and some commented that they waited up to fifteen years. Part of your career goal setting should include a timeline. Are you willing to wait around five, ten, fifteen years before you work on Broadway? And these are answers from folks who actually have been in a Broadway show!

### Are you currently employed in a Broadway show?
Yes  15 males (37%), 11 females (32%)

No  26 males (63%), 23 females (68%)

This is relevant only for the cross section of actors I was able to interview. I originally set out to interview actors working solely on Broadway but then realized that including all working actors was a more all-encompassing and realistic view of the business. The true numbers are more revealing and discouraging. There are about fifty thousand registered union actors in New York City and probably no more than a thousand jobs. The math is scary: the 2 percent of all union actors in NYC who are working have work not just in Broadway musicals but in Broadway plays and in off-Broadway plays and musicals.

### If yes, what is your weekly salary?
*(The Broadway Production Contract minimum for the 2003-2004 season was $1,354. The figures below indicated that the actors interviewed were making approximately 25 percent more than minimum on the average.)*

Male  $1,679/week on average (2010-2011 – $2,056)

Female  $1,699/week on average (2010-2011 – $2,076)

If you happen to be one of the 550 or so working Broadway actors, you would be making good money. (The Broadway minimum increases about 3 percent a year, from $1,354 per week in 2003-2004 to $1,653 per week in 2010-2011. Use this percentage to calculate future Broadway minimum figures.) If you are on a second contract with a show or are understudying roles, your salary can go up $100 to $500 per week, and if you are playing a lead you can make excellent money. One actor, who was in the *Chess* benefit for The Actors Fund, divulged that he was making $4,500 a week. He was undoubtedly playing a major lead role. On the other end of the scale, ten men and four women who answered the survey were either at Broadway minimum or within $100 of it.

### How many Broadway shows have you done?
Male

Twenty-eight men said they had done at least one Broadway show, while thirteen did not answer or replied NA. These twenty-eight were in fifty-seven total productions, an average of two each. Sixteen of the twenty-eight were in one only, four actors did two, and eight did three or more shows (four actors did three shows, two did four shows, one did six, and one did seven).

Female
Twenty-six women said they had done at least one Broadway show, while eight did not answer or replied NA. These twenty-six were in sixty-two total productions, an average of 2.4 each. Thirteen of the twenty-six were in one only, four actors did two, and nine did three or more shows (five actors did three shows, two actors did five shows, one did six shows, and one had appeared in ten shows).

How long did each show last?
Male
Fourteen months on average

Female
Eighteen months on average

There's not much to say here other than there's no such thing as job security!

## Budget

The following question came after another asking whether or not survey respondents continued to study or work out. You'll recall that 95 percent of the actors said yes.

If so, what do you spend monthly on your "studies"?
$260 ($300 in 2010-'11 dollars) was the average monthly investment

This is relevant when trying to calculate a total monthly living expense for NYC (or for any city).

Here is a possible scenario for living expenses in NYC. The first set of numbers indicates 2011 estimates. The rent estimate reflects your portion of the split with a roommate. Use a 2 percent increase for each year after to calculate ballpark budget figures.

|  | 2011 | 2016 |
|---|---|---|
| Rent including heat (w/roommate) | $590-$715 month | $650-$785 |
| Training and gym membership | $175/mo to start | $190-$195 |
| Utilities (gas/electricity) | $60/mo | $65-$70 |
| Groceries (eating out not included) | $285/mo | $315 |
| Package cable/internet/cell phone | $100-$200 | $110-$220 |
| Transportation/Metro card (per mo.) | $104 | $118 |
| Miscellaneous | $115 | $125-$130 |
| Total expenses monthly | $1,429-$1,654 | $1,573-$1,833 |

New York City is an incredible place with so much to offer, but it presents challenges as well when you live there. Rental costs, choice of where to reside (off the island probably), the tools you'll use, timing of getting your Equity card, the length of your pursuit of the dream, and living expenses are all important aspects that you'll sooner or later need to contemplate. Create a financial plan before you move to a big city. Consider working a job for a short time to save enough money to make a comfortable move. Careful planning for your relocation will allow the phrase "a helluva town" to be a positive rather than a negative one for you!

# SECTION TWO:
# Each Journey Is Unique

One of the reasons I spent a year away from teaching was to see how I would fare back in the field of musical theatre and to pursue and achieve the ultimate goal of being cast in a Broadway show. I felt that my musical theatre career was a full and satisfying one, but this was the one goal I'd contemplated yet never achieved. My most recent musical theatre job had been a European production of *Cats*, and I'd left that show in February 1994. When I arrived in NYC, nine and a half years had passed since I had done an audition, performed in a show, or taken a class, so I knew I would need some remedial training to get all of the required skills back into shape.

During my year in NYC, I tried to simulate as best I could what it would be like for a young actor moving to the city for the first time. However, I had some distinct advantages that someone directly out of college wouldn't have, and these were unavoidable. First, I had a sabbatical income (from New Trier) and although it wasn't quite enough to cover all living expenses, it kept the wolf away from the door. Second, three years of planning for the sabbatical had offered the opportunity to save a good deal of money. This helped cushion the blow of moving to the city (security deposit, rent, etc.) and helped cover expenses for acting and dance classes and voice lessons. Third, I had already had a life as a professional actor that started early in my college days and continued for nine years after I finished my undergraduate degree. And, last, I had wisdom only years can offer and a fulfilling marriage, both of which gave me an important support system.

One could argue that these were disadvantages because they took the edge off my desire to succeed. The hunger of a young actor with nothing to lose and everything to gain was not something I possessed at this point in life. Nonetheless, I have discovered there is no definitive course toward success for any one person to take. The following are two examples of this truth:

**1.** My friend Paul Castree earned a degree in psychology from the University of Illinois but decided instead to go into musical theatre as a career because he loved it and was a gifted performer. Paul has done nine Broadway shows to date. He's been extremely successful, but at one point he went through a three-year period where he found himself looking too old to play teen and young adult parts yet not old enough to play mature adult roles. He worked sporadically in this period, but it tested his resolve and he needed to reassess. Fortunately, he came out on the side of success. One thing's for sure: His most recent job will someday end and he will again be looking for work.

**2.** Shonn Wiley played Ren McCormack in the production of *Footloose* that I was in during the spring of 2004. Shonn came out of Carnegie Mellon University and went directly to NYC. Within the first couple of years he'd played several lead roles in local regional theatres and was cast in the Broadway revival of *42nd Street*. Shortly after leaving that show, he went through a spell of unemployment and was forced to take a survival job. His resolve was also tested and he contemplated other ways to make a living related to the career he'd chosen. Then toward the end of *Footloose*, he auditioned and was cast in a lead role in the new Frank Wildhorn production *Dracula*, which opened on Broadway a few months later. For one so young, Shonn was a highly successful actor, but even he had already faced a challenging time.

In the end, it just goes to show that even the most gifted and well-trained people who seem to be on a great track can struggle with unemployment and in turn lose confidence. The most important qualities to recognize in these two unique journeymen are commitment and perseverance. They continue to possess the *passion* necessary to be successful in the business of musical theatre.

# SECTION THREE:
## Journal

## Ladd in the City

As I created the sabbatical project, I sensed early on that keeping a record of my experience would be important not only for my reflection but possibly for students contemplating musical theatre as a career. The journal did prove to be highly beneficial for my own growth as an artist and person. I hope it can, in turn, help those who read it make an easier decision in regard to a career in musical theatre.

## Reflections on the Journal

Although I was incredibly excited to be in NYC and doing what I had always longed for, some realities quickly emerged:

- Auditioning can be a very difficult and frustrating experience. I'd been a professional for many years. But, in looking back, I realized I had not really had to audition a great deal and therefore had never developed a solid craft for this all-important necessity of the business. I also let the fact that I had been to New York before and had done very well in a few auditions give me a false sense of confidence. I confused a little bit of good luck and timing with ability and talent.

- It wasn't until I found a good voice teacher in the city and started taking a musical theatre audition technique class that I really felt prepared to handle an actual audition situation. Only then was I able to sit in a room with 150 other men vying for the one or two nonunion jobs in that show without struggling with nerves and confidence issues. Another thing I never quite mastered was sitting for several hours after I had vocally warmed up, then walking into a room and singing a brilliant sixteen bars cold. The best auditions I had were the ones where I was able to find a room in the same studio and rewarmed up just before auditioning.

- New York City without money in your pocket can be a depressing place. It's frustrating to know that an endless number of productions are waiting to be seen and that you can't see them! Katherine and I did see a number of shows but not to the degree we would have liked. Dining out was another luxury we could not afford, and we ate out only sparingly.

- Anybody can take out an ad in the trade paper (*Back Stage*), hold an audition, and, if they have the funds, put up a show! You don't have to be a professional or have any talent at all. I guess the lesson learned here is that just because it's advertised in *Back*

*Stage* doesn't mean it's a quality project. Do research, if possible, on the production and the people involved before committing yourself.

And finally, what follows is the journal that I kept while in New York City. In its complete form it made for some dry reading so I have included only the excerpts I thought relevant or interesting.

## JOURNAL EXCERPTS

### July

*July 1, 2003, Tuesday.*
We left Evanston, Illinois, this morning at 9:45 after a harried scramble to vacate our townhouse. We had spent the past two weeks trying to undo what took four and a half years to create. Our original departure time was 8:30 a.m. but a plethora of issues would not allow it. It was a blessing in disguise, however, because as we got on the Edens Expressway heading south (or east, as the sign deceivingly said), the traffic was light. Ah, the first lesson about moving to New York City in a truck: Leave town at an hour that doesn't leave you a tense wreck on the freeway battling traffic in a monstrous vehicle.

Once on the highway, Lance (the thirteen-year-old cat), who had been emitting some incredibly painful and sorrowful meows, began to settle down. Because of his advanced age, we'd opted for the nontranquilized trip, and we're glad we did because he wouldn't have handled those drugs very well. All in all, he fared the trip quite bravely. Katherine and I traded off driving responsibilities and took I-80 all the way to Youngstown, Ohio (travel time eight hours). A thriving metropolis on the Pennsylvania border, Youngstown offered a clean, cool, affordable Best Western that had a decent restaurant, Winston's, right on the premises. This was a good thing because we then had a nice, quiet dinner with some good wine on our ninth wedding anniversary. That's right, we spent our anniversary in the cab of a Penske Truck. Other than enduring Lance's constant pacing about the strange hotel room, we slept well.

*July 2, Wednesday.*
By the way, I won't necessarily be keeping a daily journal. Eventually it will probably take the form of a weekly. But while I'm still in the mood ... Day Two of the journey was basically uneventful as is most of the middle of Pennsylvania. We made another McDonald's pit stop, this one in a place we both knew that if we found ourselves growing up there, the first thing we'd want to do is get out. Seven hours after our departure, we arrived in Hackensack, New Jersey. Those of you unfamiliar with New Jersey will be pleased to know that Hackensack is just across the Hudson River from the northern tip of Manhattan (our destination). The Hackensack Best Western was a little

less clean, cool, and affordable than the one in Youngstown but was functional for what we needed. The in-house restaurant was an outrageously priced Japanese place so we opted for a jaunt across the street to a TGIF. Once again pacing, Lance hampered slightly our attempts at sleep, but we managed to garner enough shuteye for...

*July 3, Thursday.*

The Big Day! We got up this morning and had a somewhat insufficient "continental breakfast" in the lobby of the hotel, where people were walking past with all their clanky luggage and complaining children. It was OK because our minds were on greater things. We hustled back to the room, grabbed up our things (including Lance), and made our way to the truck. Thankfully it hadn't been vandalized in the night. Yeah, we were out of that parking lot, out of New Jersey, and on our way to the city.

Well, in order to get to Manhattan from any location you have to either cross a monstrous bridge or use one of the tunnels, each of which costs a significant toll. In our case it was the George Washington Bridge, which was six dollars. As we approached we found ourselves in the wrong lanes. We wound up in an E-ZPass lane for cars and couldn't back out because other E-ZPass users were waiting and honking behind us. Not knowing what to do, we just started driving through and a cop on the side of the road screamed at us to pull over. He accused us of purposely running a toll and really gave us a hard time for a good ten minutes. We finally convinced him that we were just two lost idiots from Chicago trying to get to our new apartment, and he let us go.

From there we got lost only one more time before making it to our neighborhood—and our getting lost gave us an opportunity to drive through Tryon Park, a beautiful botanical garden. Once in the neighborhood, we found the apartment quickly, and within a few minutes (and a few times around the block) had a place to park right outside the place. Katherine found Bella (the landlady), and the guys who were to unload the truck were right on time. Three hours later we were sitting in the apartment with all our stuff. We'd made it!

One of the first things we did outside the apartment was walk down to the Chinese takeout for some wonderful food. (There's no place in Evanston—or anywhere on the North Shore of Chicago, for that matter—that has good quality, cheap Chinese food and will actually deliver.) It being summer, we opted for takeout.

*July 4, Friday.*

Fourth of July. Needless to say, we didn't participate in any festivities today. We spent the day unpacking and that was about it.

*July 11, Friday.*

The last week was spent doing a number of different necessary errands and tasks. Unpacking and setting up our apartment was no small job. However, the details are boring so I won't elaborate.

I just joined a gym (the YMCA at 63rd Street and Central Park West) and I will start to take dance a couple of times a week at a studio that Katherine knows well called Dance Space Center, down on Canal Street. DSC is a nice alternative to Steps and Broadway Dance, which are known for being notoriously overcrowded.

I'm signed up for a soap opera class starting in August, to be taught by a major casting director for soaps in NYC named Bob Lambert. Although I have no soap experience, it should be fun and a good experience. (As it turned out, I wasn't able to take this class because of other commitments, and Katherine took the slot instead.)

We live in a wonderfully quiet neighborhood on the northern tip of Manhattan. I can walk less than a block and be at four small grocery stores, one large grocery, a florist, a video store, any number of dry cleaners and coin laundries, a hardware store, several restaurants, a drugstore, a pet care place, and a branch of Chase Bank. Another half block and I have a spectacular view of the Hudson River. Also, a block's walk away is a subway stop for the A train, an express train that can get me downtown in 15 minutes. I'm incredibly blessed to have such an oasis.

*July 12, Saturday.*
Audition #1. Audition for *The Kid Who Played the Palace*. The audition ran from 10 a.m. to 7 p.m., and union actors were given preference when they arrived. I arrived about 10:25 and finally auditioned about 1:30. The rest of my time was spent in reluctant conversations with mothers of young girls who were there to audition. The holding pen was a small theatrical space that was air-conditioned to within an inch of its life. After about an hour in that icebox I moved, out into the hall at first and then finally into the waiting room outside the audition room. The longer I sat, the bolder I became about finding out exactly what was going on and when I would be auditioning.

Sitting in the waiting room outside the audition room was interesting because I got to see and hear how this audition was run. The production team was the writer/director/producer Peter Sklar, a woman who sat at the table with him, and a woman who was the accompanist. Their assistants were eight girls, all about sixteen to eighteen years old, who I later learned were a part of some educational experience with the producer. This audition was a workshop for them to learn how to run an audition. In that regard it was highly unprofessionally run. However, there was no denying the talent of the kids who were walking through the door to audition. Some came out with sides (dialogue from the show) to read and some were dismissed.

I finally walked through the door and truly had a moment of nearly uncontrollable nervousness because it had been so long since I'd done an audition! I held it together and made my way first to the table to drop off my pic and resume and then to the piano to discuss my song selections. I had decided to sing "I Won't Send Roses" and "I Don't Remember Christmas." I had transposed "...Roses," in freehand, to a lead sheet to get it into a range for my voice, but not all accompanists are comfortable reading handwritten lead sheets. I showed it to the pianist; she was fine with it but said that in order to stay under the "thirty seconds per song" requirement that I needed to start halfway through. I hadn't sung since I'd warmed up at nine that morning, and I had only a phrase and a half before the high G to get warmed up again. It was a bit bumpy and I felt as stiff as a board, but I managed to get to the end of the song. I went straight into the second song and did better with this but was still feeling stiff.

My experience with the director was noteworthy. Just before I sang, he asked what part I was auditioning for, as though there wasn't anything in the show for my age range. For a second I panicked, thinking I had misread the info, but said "Bob Monroe?" Then they said, "Oh yes, of course, we put Bob in the listing!"

After I sang he was very inquisitive about what I'd been up to and why I decided to return to performing. He asked if he could give me some advice and then told me that my pics made me look too old! He said I looked fifty! So I gave him my other, more serious shot and he said, "It's better, but you still look older in the pic than you do in person." I said thanks and then he said they'd be in touch, whatever that means. I'm not holding my breath for a response from them, but it was a very interesting experience.

*July 13, Sunday.*
Day of rest. Starbucks, cafe au lait, *NYTimes*, trip to Borders for books, work on the apartment (in kitchen), watched the movie *Maid in Manhattan*. We saw an old friend in the movie named Ton Voogt, who was a fellow cast member of ours in *Cats*. He played the intense Dutch Pilates instructor—which happens to be his nationality and current occupation.

*July 15, Tuesday*
Today was the fifth time in the last eight days that I've worked out and at the end of the day I am starting to feel it. Although I've worked out over the last years I haven't sustained any kind of intense regiment. It will be interesting to see how well my forty-one-year-old body holds up.

I had a major breakthrough today with my voice. I have been singing every day since I've arrived in NYC and I've slowly been building stamina. In the past month, I've been practicing the exercises that I'd worked on with Daniel Kane, my Chicago voice teacher, and things were going pretty well. Yesterday, I was a little disappointed in that I was fatigued after just a few phrases of "Lonely House." Today while working on the flip exercise (flipping back and forth between falsetto and chest) I remembered to hold my jaw down as far as it would go. This had a major impact on my upper range and some jaw tension was obviously released. Before the adjustment, I was holding the jaw but not in the extreme lowest position. While doing that, high G and A-flat came out well, but when I went back down to F-sharp I really struggled. That's when I tried the full extension and, boom, it immediately released and the sound was full and completely free. I noticed that at the same time my support became more resolute. After finishing both F-sharp and F, I rested and then worked on the last few phrases of "Lonely House." I worked first in singing some phrases in vocal fry (an exercise where the vocal folds are brought together loosely, allowing air to bubble through, resulting in a rattling quality of vocal sound) and then in full voice. Then I went back and sang from "I guess there must be something I don't comprehend..." and sang to the end with almost no fatigue or effect. I was so excited!

*July 17, Thursday.*

Much has happened since I last wrote. I was offered the opportunity to workshop several roles, including Bob Monroe, in *The Kid Who Played the Palace* and will start rehearsing on Sunday! The phone call from the producer was such a shock to receive because I never thought I would get called from the very first audition I did here. It was supposed to be for practice only. Anyway, no need for too much excitement, it doesn't pay and there's not even a performance scheduled yet!

Audition #2. Yesterday, I auditioned for *There's A Marquee...* and felt much better about the experience. I almost didn't do it because it involved script reading right from the start and I am particularly rusty at that. But I thought it would be a good "class" for me and decided to go for it. I ended up reading a half dozen times and although I didn't feel especially good about it, I just kept trying to improve. The man running the audition was very nice, which helped a lot. I then sang and I thought it went well. After singing I had one more opportunity to read and finally had the chance to read the sides that I'd had a few minutes to look at before the audition began. (The other sides were completely cold readings!) This last read was my strongest and afterward the person running the audition seemed excited and said he'd be in touch. Again, I won't be holding my breath, but it was nice to have such a successful audition.

Katherine and I had our anniversary last night (This is our other anniversary. We got married twice; once in a private ceremony July 1 and the other time to have a big party!) and went out on the town. We had dinner at a nice restaurant and then went next door to the St. James Theatre and saw *The Producers* ($100 a ticket). We had a great time and knew two people in the cast, with whom we chatted afterward. John Egan was Old Deuteronomy in *Cats* Zurich and was playing a major role in the show. He was excellent. Also, Brad Musgrove, an old friend from my Opryland and cruise ship days, was in the show playing Carmen Ghia. He's been in the show since day one and has a great gig. He's on for only seventeen minutes and is also dance captain. What a job! The show was really quite wonderful but we were a little disappointed with the two men who were cast in the Nathan Lane and Matthew Broderick roles. They just seemed to be copying rather than doing their own interpretations of the roles.

*July 21, Monday.*

I now have two jobs! I was cast in *There's a Marquee....* I'll be understudying one of the leads and playing a smaller role. This show actually has dates and will be an Equity showcase running August 29 to September 7. Again, another show "trying to go to Broadway," although this one has already had a life and, with dates confirmed in a space off-Broadway, a strong effort is being made there. I start on the 30th.

*July 22, Tuesday.*

We saw *Rhapsody in Seth* last night. Seth Rudetsky is a close friend of Paul Castree, who is a close friend of mine! This is a one-man show written by Seth and is largely autobiographical. Seth has played the piano in the pit for many Broadway shows and is also a stand-up comic. He wrote for Rosie O'Donnell's TV show. It was a funny show but had enough poignant moments that made the comic relief all the more effective. (As of 2011, Seth is still in the thick of all that is Broadway. Check out his website at *sethrudetsky.com*.)

*July 23, Wednesday.*

I went to the first read-through of *The Kid Who Played the Palace* last night. It was a very interesting evening. I showed up around 6:45 (early as usual) because the rehearsal was supposed to start at 7:00. Most of the actors were on time but the director walked in at 7:05 and the rest of his help didn't arrive until 7:30. They were to supply the necessary items such as SCRIPTS. It had been raining so the scripts were all damp and wrinkly. Then the director passed around a sheet for contact information and wanted to wait until after it had been finished before we started with the read-through, so that wasted another half-hour! We finally got started at 8:00. I guess you can tell from the tone of my writing that I have a certain expectation regarding professionalism. If I had done that for the first read-through of a show at New Trier, the place would have been up for grabs.

I still can't tell if the show has any potential because I haven't heard any of the music. (That, also, was not a part of the first rehearsal.) The story is a nice one, though, and seems to have some possibilities. I'm still not aware of what exactly I'll be doing in the show. When I was originally cast I was told I'd be in one number that takes place in the Actors' Equity lounge, but when we got to that part of the read-through, the director had other people read it. I think it's because I had read a number of other roles by that point and he was trying to pass around opportunity in the read-through. So, this is a chance for me to learn as much as I can in the situation that's been presented and learn more about the meaning of the word flexibility.

On my way home I heard again from Leon Davis, the man who wrote, choreographed, and directs *There's a Marquee...*, the other show that I will be in. He informed me that I have been promoted and will be playing the role of one of the judges, which is more significant with more time onstage, lots of singing, movement, etc. Again, I'm a bit wary about his organizational skills—he ran the whole audition by himself—but at least the show has a limited run and it could yield some great results for me personally.

Today I took my first yoga class ever, at the YMCA, and I'm trying to recover from it. It was Iyanger yoga and, other than the first position, which put some pressure on my hip, it was all doable for me. Katherine and I were very different in the specific positions that we could execute effectively. She's always been flexible in her legs and hips, and my former training in gymnastics helped me with certain balance positions. (As it turned out, I attended only two yoga sessions and found it to be a little too static for my body. I ended up opting for dance class instead.)

*July 26, Saturday.*
I was pleased to see Christy Faeber, Emily Shoolin, and Liza Miller, all New Trier alums, in the past week. They're all living here in the city, trying to work in the business. Emily is about to go back out on the road with TheatreWorks, where she started last fall and got her Equity card. Christy also got her card last fall working at Goodspeed, a regional theatre in Connecticut, and just finished playing Gloria Upson in *Mame* at North Shore Dinner Theatre in Boston. They've both done quite well so far considering that they're really very young. Liza just graduated from New York University and is working as a waitress this summer. She's taking a short break before delving into her career in the fall. It was great to see them and have that connection to New Trier.

# August

*August 2, Saturday.*
I had my first rehearsal last night for *Marquee...* and can hardly move today. We rehearsed choreography for about two hours and it's all very aerobic stuff. The difficulty level of the movement was not high but the cardiovascular aspect is. I was good for about ninety minutes but we had to repeat the movement so many times that I just got worn out. I thought I was getting into good shape but apparently not! I play the role of a judge who's got a major attitude. You might say that I'm the comic relief in the show, which I kind of like. It's a very simplistic story and of another era. Very innocent and family oriented. It will run at the American Theatre for Actors on West Fifty-fourth Street about a block and a half from Broadway.

Katherine and I are both going to sing in a benefit for the Actors Fund at the end of September. During the early part of this summer my friend Paul Castree (mentioned July 22) told me about his experience the previous year performing in the annual Actors Fund benefit of *Funny Girl*. He wasn't going to be able to do this year's upcoming performance because he was out of town working in a regional theatre but thought I should do it. He called his good friend Seth Rudetsky (also mentioned July 22), who is the artistic director of the benefit, reminded him of me (I'd met him previously and actually had a coaching session with him years earlier) and suggested he cast not only me but also Katherine. Seth was delighted and more than willing to have us join the cast.

The show is a concert version of *Chess*, which will be a blast especially for Katherine (she was in the original Broadway company). The two male leads are high-profile singers. One is Adam Pascal, who originated the role of Roger Davis in *Rent* and went on to star in Elton John's *Aida*. The other guy, whose name slips my mind (Josh somebody), has recently done a major TV special and was on *Ally McBeal* playing himself. He's an amazing singer and you've probably seen him. (Turned out to be a guy named Josh Groban, who has done pretty well for himself since working with me.) Anyway, it should be fun, it's a great cause, and there is the added bonus of making connections.

I have two auditions coming up in the next few weeks. One is for *Swing*, which is exactly how it sounds: A show that takes place in the forties with swing dancing. I'm a little cautious about trying it because of physical shape issues, but I may just go and see what happens. The other is for *A Tree Grows in Brooklyn* and seems a little more up my alley (less crazy dancing). They're both in local regional theatres and both offer Equity cards to nonunion actors.

*August 3, Sunday.*

We've been in New York for exactly a month and things are beginning to feel settled. The apartment is finally put together the way we like it and it works for us for the most part. (You can always use a little more storage space!) Lance is adjusting slowly but spends quite a bit of time in my closet. It's dark, quiet and safe in there. He comes out to eat and visit. I figured out a way to pump cool air from the window unit air conditioner in our bedroom to the rest of the apartment using a series of fans. It's been really hot here. Our neighborhood is a friendly place and we use all the local stores for our needs. We walk to everything.

I'm struggling with going from having every second of my day planned for me as a teacher to having literally weeks ahead with hardly anything on the menu. It's so foreign to me and I must admit I don't like the feeling. I feel guilty every time I have some free time and don't fill it with something career-oriented. When I was teaching, it felt good to take a few minutes or hours here or there. I need to cut myself some slack because I didn't have a vacation before moving here. I worked at New Trier right up to the end and then frantically prepared to move to NYC. Even when I first got here, I jumped right into doing auditions knowing I needed to make the most of my time. Now I'm trying to slow down a little and it's freaking me out.

So I took today and didn't do anything work-wise (except this journal entry).

*August 5, Tuesday.*

Audition #3. Yesterday I auditioned for *Swing* and held up pretty well considering it was a dancer-only call. I don't know what I was doing there because I was probably at least ten years older than the oldest people there! Most were college age or a little older and in great shape. It was good for me to go; I treated it like another class. I've done some swing-type dancing before but many years ago and not nearly as detailed and specific as this. I really struggled the whole time with "Should I be here?" which I think affected my ability to go for it. It was good because I need to trust my instincts—and they were telling me this wasn't for me. So, as a result I tanked the audition. I actually made it through the first cut but was released after the second.

Later in the day I had two rehearsals that conflicted with each other and I was really panicked that one of the directors would be upset with me. I called them both and let them know that I'd have to leave one early and come late to the other. As it turned out, there was absolutely no need to feel that way because each rehearsal was so loosely run. Neither of the directors even mentioned my phone call.

The first was for *Kid Who Played the Palace* and I waited a half-hour for my rehearsal to start. During this time Peter Sklar, the director, was welcoming a new crew of kids to the show and then had an older woman audition for a part. Apparently, he's double- and triple-casting the kids and still looking for more people to do the staged readings. Finally, we worked on my scene, the "Actors' Equity Lounge," and it really is a good one. The music is pretty sophisticated. He fancies it to be what Sondheim would have written in the 1930s. It went well and we finished thirty minutes early, which gave me plenty of time to get to the other rehearsal. (Midtown to Washington Square at Sixth Street and Lafayette, about a twenty-minute subway ride.)

I got there a few minutes early and ended up waiting another half-hour! The *Marquee...* rehearsal was primarily scene work and then a quick review of choreography we'd done the week before. I'd worked on it quite a bit but thought I might still not be ready enough for the director. Again, my hunch was wrong as he struggled remembering it himself! The other guy hadn't worked on it at all so I was the one refreshing their memories on the movement. We rehearsed until about 11:00 and then talked in the hall about the new schedule. It then took me almost an hour and a half to get home because the trains were running really late. I was so burned when I finally crawled into bed at 1:00 a.m.

*August 9, Saturday.*

Katherine and I met Karen Hall (a former colleague from Mundelein High School who now teaches at Maine East High School in Park Ridge, Illinois) in midtown today to see a production of *Big River*. I think it was the most beautiful show I have ever seen, and that says a lot. It was produced by Roundabout Theatre Company and Deaf West Theatre (out of LA) and it was created for both hearing and hard-of-hearing audiences. Some cast members were deaf or hard of hearing, while others were hearing, and the entire show was signed. The show was beautifully crafted, from the highly versatile set, to the period costumes, to the sign-language-enhanced choreography. There was something very compelling about having the music and singing enhanced by the signing. It was as if having that additional form of expression enabled the actors to go deeper into their emotional selves. Absolutely fantastic.

*August 15, Friday.*

Yesterday I was taking a nap in the afternoon and woke up when the air conditioner shut off. I thought we'd probably blown a fuse but then I noticed the entire apartment was out. Katherine and I ventured into the hallway only to find the elevator not working. The entire building was out! We got curious and walked down the five flights of stairs to discover that the entire neighborhood was out of power. As time passed we learned that the Northeast of the U.S. and large parts of Canada had experienced a blackout.

Without any idea of how long it would last, neighbors rushed the local grocery and bought up the essentials in great haste. However, the neighborhood became unified and people were out on the sidewalk listening to battery-powered radios and checking in on the elderly. One woman had been stranded in the elevator that brings people up from the subway and had to be lifted out through the trap door in the elevator car's ceiling. She was smeared from head to foot with grease.

Our apartment grew quite hot in a short period of time but we had no other recourse except to open all of the windows and ride it out. Last evening we went up onto the roof of the building to catch a cool breeze and observed Manhattan and the surrounding boroughs in total darkness, save the nearby hospital running on reserve power. It was almost surreal to be able to observe stars while on the island! Two couples in our building had it right when they had their dinner by candlelight on the rooftop.

This morning at about 8:45 the power came back on. We were so relieved to have our conveniences again. The thing that stood out most to me was the way people in the neighborhood took care of each other. It was apparent that 9/11 had had a profound effect on them all.

*August 18, Monday.*

Audition #4. I auditioned today for *A Tree Grows In Brooklyn* for Goodspeed Musicals and sang sixteen bars of "Come Back To Me." I didn't sing well and felt poorly about it afterward. I was very nervous and didn't support my voice. Not a good audition.

*August 20, Wednesday.*

Audition #5. I auditioned for Westchester Broadway Theatre, a dinner theatre up in Westchester County. The show was *Miracle on 34th Street* and I sang "Sometimes a Day Goes By." Again I sang poorly, which was shocking. I have been singing this song for fifteen years and always do well with it. I find that I choke when I get in front of a table of directors. Ahhh!

Today was the first *Chess* rehearsal. It took place in one of the Actors Fund's spaces, a fairly large room with a baby grand and many chairs set up in chorus style. Most folks were on time, and Catherine Cooke, the director of these activities for the Actors Fund, started it off by thanking us for volunteering and then made some introductions. The important person, of course, was Seth Rudetsky, who was the artistic producer and musical director of the benefit. He proceeded to lead us through a somewhat grueling rehearsal of the big chorus numbers in the show. It was fun to sit amongst some of Broadway's finest entertainers. Lots of talent in the room.

*August 28, Thursday.*
Katherine and I went to the U.S. Open Tennis Championships today in Flushing Meadows, New York. It was something we'd always wanted to do. We saw some incredible tennis and were blown away at the intensity and pace of the game. Watching professionals on TV and in person is two totally different things. We then walked around and took in matches on other courts. The most interesting was Juan Carlos Ferrerro on the Grandstand court. He had lost the first set but came back to win it in four. He's a very exciting player to watch and we were so close to the action.

We had to hurry back from Queens so I could get to my final dress rehearsal for *There's A Marquee...* It is in no way near ready for an audience, I'm afraid. We'll see how it goes. The show opens tomorrow night and will run for ten performances through Sunday, September 7.

*August 30, Saturday.*
*There's A Marquee...* had its opening last night and fortunately there was a pretty small audience. The set is still not finished and there are a myriad of other technical issues, from sound to lighting. Fortunately, there are other wonderful Broadway shows for my father to see when he arrives on Friday!

*August 31, Sunday.*
We decided to go one more time to the U.S. Open because we learned that Andre Agassi's match with Yevgani Kafelnikov was rained out yesterday and that it would be finished today. We've always wanted to see him so we bought a couple of scalped tickets. We saw him demolish Kafelnikov in straight sets, then watched a bit as Andy Roddick creamed an unseeded player. What an opportunity for us!

# September

*September 3, Wednesday.*

Audition #6. Paper Mill Playhouse held auditions today for *The Sound of Music*. I thought that I was perfect for this show with my fair looks but it turned out they were heading in a youth direction. Apparently they didn't see me as a character type to play supporting roles. I was typed out.

*September 5, Friday.*

My dad arrived today from Spring Green, Wisconsin. He hasn't been in New York for about twenty years but was here many times in the sixties and seventies while chaperoning high school groups. He had a good flight and we took him for dinner to our favorite neighborhood restaurant, 187 West, prior to my call for *There's A Marquee....* It was great to see him.

*September 7, Sunday.*

Audition #7. Just yesterday I heard word of mouth about a show called *Loud* by a small company named Curtain Call. The show is an edgy rock opera and they were looking for a man to play a slightly older man in the show. They were heading toward an off-Broadway run after a success during the summer at the Fringe Festival. I sang well ("I Chose Right" and "Lost in the Wilderness") but, alas, I was not what they were looking for. Directly after the audition I had to run to my call for the last performance of *There's a Marquee....*

*September 8, Monday.*

*There's a Marquee...* is finally over and not a moment too soon. The worst piece of theatre I've ever been involved in! About two weeks before the production was to go up, I began to have doubts about its viability. Leon just couldn't seem to get it together; he tried to do too much. A few key people dropped out and the rehearsal process was very haphazard. When we finally got into the space, it became painfully obvious that the show was doomed. Leon enlisted his reluctant children to tech the show. We didn't have a set to work with until the day before the show went up, and most things such as lighting, sound, and costumes didn't come together until the night the show opened. Simply unprofessional. UNPROFESSIONAL!!!!!

The director was also the composer, lyricist, librettist, choreographer, set designer, costumer, producer, and star! You can see where that was going. The man was stretched too thin and didn't ask for help. I did manage, however, to get an off-Broadway credit on my resume, and a casting consultant was very interested in me after the show. I think he'll be able to offer some good counsel. I made some nice friends and am happily moving on.

*September 9, Tuesday.*

My father left today after his brief stay with us. He saw *There's a Marquee...* on Saturday night (he was actually very forgiving of the show and thought my performance rose above its amateur nature), saw a couple of others (*Chicago* and *Thoroughly Modern Millie*), and had a great time. We dined out a few times, and once I met him in Times Square—under the statue by the TKTS booths—after my show and the one he saw (*Millie*). The city was absolutely buzzing and I know he loves it here. He said he'll probably return in the spring.

*September 11, Thursday.*

Today I met with Bob Luke, the casting consultant who witnessed *There's a Marquee....* He had a lot of advice but not much time because of an overburdened schedule. He looked at my resume and gave me some suggestions for changes. He also said I should buy a *Ross Report* and then make another appointment with him to go over which agencies to pursue for representation. He was very big on TV and said I should be pursuing that as well.

*September 16, Tuesday.*

Josh Groban was at the rehearsal yesterday. What a voice for a twenty-two-year-old! He's quite the talent and so nice and unaffected.

I was talking to a guy in my section and told him I was from Chicago and taught at New Trier. He said, "Well then, do you know Adam Hunter sitting over there?" Adam was a 1990 New Trier graduate who at the time participated in choir-opera (my musical theatre class). I thought I had recognized him but couldn't put a name with the face. He's in the featured ensemble with Katherine and he sounds great. A really high, focused tenor voice. I will reintroduce myself to him at Saturday's rehearsal.

*September 22, Monday.*

My mother came into town from Wisconsin on Friday to see the benefit and visit for a while. Although she struggles with her bad back, she was game to do some exploring of the city. We rented a wheelchair and went downtown last night to see *Thoroughly Modern Millie*. It was fun to see Sutton Foster in the starring role and in a completely different light than the role of *Chess'* dark Svetlana. She has impeccable timing and truly commands the stage. I'm afraid the show wouldn't be quite the same without her star quality, but it's a very tightly run piece with a high level of professionalism.

*September 23, Tuesday.*

The *Chess* benefit last night was wonderful. Katherine was in the featured ensemble and I in the chorus. Try to imagine the most fantastic Broadway theatre, the New Amsterdam on Forty-second Street, with a full audience, cast members from every Broadway show, plus dignitaries like Rosie O'Donnell and the actual creators of the show (Tim Rice,

Bjorn Ulvaeus, and Benny Andersen of *Mamma Mia* fame) all showering praise on the actors onstage. That is what it was like and it was a real high. The performance raised $800,000 for the Actors Fund, which is an organization that gives assistance to thespians in need.

The party afterward was interesting. Josh Groban has a middle-aged female following and they were trying to buy scalped tickets to the post-performance party! Some were able to get in and they were so crazy weird, stealing his wine glass and napkin after he used them. Truly bizarre.

*September 29, Monday.*
Audition #8. I went to an open call today for *Hairspray* for future replacements of the Broadway and national touring companies. This was definitely what is known as a "cattle call." I got there an hour and a half before the audition started and was 415 on the list. Two hundred had camped out overnight on the sidewalk! The line was outside and went around one full city block! I waited outside in the rain for four hours. When I was about to go through the door to the audition, the line behind me was longer than when I had gotten into it. They had four separate rooms going and would allow only sixteen bars of music. Two high school kids before me got called back. They're literally looking for high school kids sixteen to eighteen years old. I auditioned for an older role but I don't think I was what they wanted. Paul said it's also a big publicity stunt for the show. The media arrive with cameras and report on all those people waiting to audition for *Hairspray,* which is great exposure for the show. (This audition was the only open call I attended in the year I was in NYC. Although it was an eye-opening experience, I realized that I never wanted to go through that again!)

# October

*October 2, Thursday.*
*The Kid Who Played the Palace* is in workshop mode and will be giving some staged readings soon. It's a musical about an elderly vaudeville actor who tries to save NYC's old theaters from the wrecking ball. It's quite charming and has a very nice score. We will be making a CD, and Bravo is following one of the actors to do a show on what his life is like. I'm not sure when it will be broadcast but you may be able to see me in the background or working in a scene. (The show became *Showbiz Moms and Dads* and the actor was Duncan Nutter. A clip I found on YouTube didn't include anything from my musical.)

*October 4, Saturday.*
Audition #9. A few days ago I called a woman who'd been suggested to me for voice lessons (Judith Fredricks). I didn't hear from her for two days and I thought I'd have to keep looking. Then yesterday she called out of the blue. After a brief conversation she asked if I was interested in auditioning for an opera showcase "heading for Broadway."

Apparently, it's a new version of *Die Fledermaus (The Bat)* in English. I had nothing to lose so I went. I met her in this little theatre in the Village where she listened to me sing and then proceeded to give me a voice lesson right on the spot. She thought I wasn't right for the part because my voice is too pop-sounding but she said she'd consider it because I have the "look" she wanted. I have a lesson with her on Wednesday and she's going to see then if I can handle it. Whatever happens happens.

*October 6, Monday.*
Today I went to the gym, then to an Office Depot on Forty-first Street and Broadway, and then to the office of the Actors Fund to pick up a "goodie bag" that each cast member of *Chess* received. It has a T-shirt, hat, poster, program, and letter from the *Chess* benefit. Very classy.

Tomorrow I will be attempting to get a mass mailing out to several agencies asking for representation. Wednesday I have a voice lesson with my new teacher and have no idea how it will go! Thursday I have an audition in the morning and an evening rehearsal for *The Kid Who Played the Palace*. Then it's Friday and another week is gone!

*October 7, Tuesday.*
Many students at New Trier have kept in touch with me and have inquired as to whether they should come and see me in a show. *The Kid Who Played the Palace* is not quite "road-trip" worthy as of yet but I will keep them informed. It has a beautiful score and a great plot, but the thing is moving toward production in a very tortoise-like fashion. Hopefully, I will still be here when it gets to that point.

*October 8, Wednesday.*
I had my first official lesson today with Judith Fredricks. After a very shaky and awkward start, I actually had a wonderful lesson. With some specific details and instruction she moved me away from a nasalized resonance to one that is directed in the teeth with an open throat. It took almost a half-hour for her to help me find the place that she wanted, but once there my voice grew dramatically and I was able to sing in the tenor range (E, F, F-sharp, G, A-flat) with lots of volume and not much fatigue. We did absolutely no work in falsetto. The jury is still out but I can't argue with results.

*October 9, Thursday.*
Audition #10. I auditioned for a production of *The Music Man* today at Chelsea Studios. The group holding the audition was the Helen Hayes Theatre Company. I thought that this would be a great show for me because I could easily either sing in the quartet or at least be a good member of the townspeople ensemble. But, alas, I gave a horrendous audition. I sang the last sixteen bars of "Her Face" and bombed by starting very poorly, stopping, and starting again! I have never done that in my life! I truly felt like the biggest amateur in the world. I'm not in a good mood!

*October 11, Saturday.*
Katherine saw an advertisement in *Back Stage* for a musical theatre audition technique class that is taught by a man she worked with years ago in the original company of *Chess*. I'm going to inquire about the class because I'm inventing new and exciting ways to suck at auditioning.

*October 13, Monday.*
I just heard back from Paul Harman about Musical Theatre Audition Technique and will be auditing the class (with Katherine) next Monday. After my initial request for information (price, times, etc.), the following correspondence occurred:

> *David,*
> *I'm always reticent when it comes to talking price by keyboard, but I cannot, in good conscience, avoid such a direct request for information. The next session will begin in the first week of November. [I strongly encourage you to audit one of my classes (at no charge) so that you can see firsthand what I do and how I do it.] The cost for a six-class session is $360.00.*
>
> *That answers your questions, but we haven't begun to address mine. What are you looking for? What's your experience been with other teachers? Are you working now? Are you auditioning now? What are you singing at your auditions these days, if you are? And there are many, many more. All of which is my way of suggesting that we talk about all this. May I suggest that you e-mail a phone number where I may reach you (I usually get cell phone numbers, which are great) or you can leave it for me on my voice mail at \*\*\*-\*\*\*-\*\*\*\*.*
>
> *Thanks again for your interest.*
> *Paul*

My response on the same day is as follows:

> *Paul,*
> *Thanks for your quick response to my e-mail and for answering my questions. I have recently returned to the business after teaching music and musical theatre in a high school for the past nine years. I'm finding myself to be extremely rusty in audition situations and feel the need to rehone my skills. I've been here about three months and have done about ten auditions so far and have not felt as though I have performed well.*
>
> *I'd gladly have a conversation with you to talk in more detail. I'm also very interested in auditing your class. My wife is also interested in the class and is someone you know. Katherine Lynne Condit was in Chess and moved here with me to once again pursue work. Would it be possible for us both to audit the class? My cell phone number is \*\*\*-\*\*\*-\*\*\*\*.*
> *David*

*October 15, Wednesday.*

Audition #11. I attended an audition today for *Guys and Dolls* at Nola Studios. I had second thoughts about this audition because it was for the Fireside Theatre in Fort Atkinson, Wisconsin, about thirty-five miles from my hometown of Waukesha. The thought of leaving New York City in the middle of the winter to go to Wisconsin was not very appealing. However, I decided to look at it as just another audition for experience's sake. I got dressed in my best gangster outfit—black pants, maroon turtleneck, and maroon plaid jacket—and proceeded to the audition. After sitting around for quite a while and marveling at the number of people who'd shown up for the audition, I got called into the room with about ten others for a typing. After we introduced ourselves, they kept three people and let the rest of us go, including me. I guess I was not what they had in mind for the forties *Guys and Dolls* gangster. Although I was upset that the remote Fireside passed me up, I was relieved I never had to make a decision about having to spend the winter in the Frozen Tundra.

*October 21, Tuesday.*

Audition #12. I auditioned for a nonunion tour of *Titanic* today at Shetler Studios. The production company is Candlewood International LLC and the director is John Hodge. Again, I didn't really want to go out on a tour with a nonunion show but I thought it would be good for me to have the audition practice. The audition notice asked for a Maury Yeston song, of which I had none, so I went to Colony (a music store in Times Square where you can find pretty much any piece of Broadway sheet music published) and found a cycle that he had written called "December Songs." Although I believe the cycle was written for a woman, many of the songs were non-gender-specific. I picked one called "Please Let's Not Even Say Hello" and worked it up in literally two days. (Not smart; I was not taking the advice I so freely hand out to my own students!) It was a very demanding song as far as range was concerned and definitely a stretch for me. I got into the waiting room and sat for a long time before finally getting to my time. By this point I was vocally cold, nervous about a new song, and nervous about an audition, in addition to not really wanting to do this job. Guess what? I tanked it. It was the most horrendous audition I've ever done. My voice could barely function at the end because I was squeezing so hard to get the high notes out. Awful!!!

*October 22, Wednesday.*

Excerpts from a letter I wrote my mother:

> *Hi Mom,*
> *I've been thinking about you a lot lately. I'm sorry about the Packers. They weren't broadcast here last week but I saw the disappointing score.*
>
> *Things are more or less the same here. I've done a few auditions but have not sung as*

*well as I'd like. We're both a little frustrated right now but that's part of the experience I asked for. I have found a voice teacher to study with, and Katherine and I are going to start taking a musical theatre audition class. Hopefully it will yield some results in the near future. I've also started taking a dance class. It's a lot of work but I enjoy it. It's a very advanced beginner class in what's called Simonson technique. It's a specific type of modern jazz and is really wonderful for the body. Katherine takes the intermediate of the same technique.*

*I've been painting my friend Tim Schultheis' apartment as payment for doing my headshots. It always takes a little longer than you think.*

*I hope you are feeling well. Thanks for keeping me up to date on the family. I love to hear about everyone's successes and endeavors. Keep writing!*

*Love,*
*David*

*October 26, Sunday.*
This was an e-mail I sent to the cast of *There's A Marquee*:

*Hi All,*
*Just wanted to let you know that I have "discovered" a great musical theatre audition class. It's called "Musical Theatre Audition Technique" and it's taught by a guy named Paul Harman, who has some fifteen Broadway shows and seven original casts to his credit. I audited the class last week and it looks really good. It's very relaxed and positive and for people of various levels of technique and experience.*

*I'm going to start with the class next week on Monday. If anyone is interested let me know and I can hook you up with Paul or you can check out his website at* **www.auditionsuccess.com**.

*Regards, David*

*October 28, Tuesday.*
Audition #13. I auditioned for touring productions of *I Love You, You're Perfect, Now Change* and *My Way* yesterday at Shetler Studios. It was for a company that tours primarily in Iowa. Although a union company, it's one that requires a lot of its actors: loading scenery, taking care of costumes, assisting in whatever way needed, etc. I was already in "audition-as-practice" mode for this one but after I heard about the working conditions I was even less inclined to want the job. Naturally, again, after I didn't sing my two selections ("From This Moment On" and "Her Face") as well as I'd hoped, I realized I have the tendency to find ways to sabotage myself. I'm in desperate need of this audition class with Paul Harman.

# November

*November 3, Monday.*

I had my first audition technique class with Paul Harman today and what an eye-opener. In such a short period of time I feel as though I have some tools and craft that will empower me to improve dramatically at auditioning. In a nutshell, the technique makes your audition performance as efficient and simplified as possible. It shows you where your focal point should be, eliminates needless gestures, and helps you shape your story for maximum effect by highlighting the contrasts in the song. I've got a ways to go before I master the art of it—right now it feels really awkward—but I can see where it's going. I wish I had started with this class in August!

*November 6, Thursday.*

Auditions #14 & #15. I had two auditions yesterday and really felt good about both of them for a change. The first was for a production of *Pippin* for Emelin Theatre and the second was for *Footloose* at Westchester Broadway Theatre. The *Pippin* audition started with a dance combination and I really worked hard at it. It was the first dance audition I'd done since *Swing* in August and although I've recently started taking class I'm still very rusty at picking up combinations. It was of course a very Fosse-esque style and although I can dance this style well I was a bit mentally blocked from paying attention to every detail that was required. I danced well but, alas, was cut. It was just as well because it seemed apparent that the choreographer/director was primarily casting his friends. People who were awesome in this audition ended up walking out with me.

The *Footloose* audition was one I almost didn't do, but at that point in the day I figured I had nothing to lose. It required sixteen bars of a pop song, which I didn't have, but I went with "Lost in the Wilderness," hoping to get to the point where I would be able to sing. The notice called for someone to play the roles of Wes Warnicker and a cop, someone a little older than the teen chorus, so I decided I might be right for it. Just before the audition, I was waiting in the studio and Katherine joined me so I could show her the dance combo for the *Pippin* audition that she was attending that afternoon. As we were working in the hallway, Barry McNabb, an old friend of Katherine's from her days in the national tour of *A Chorus Line*, recognized her on his way out for a cigarette. She introduced me and then they had a brief conversation. He is the director for this *Footloose*.

The audition started with a dance combination and this one was a little easier. It was eighties disco and country, with which I'm familiar! It had a few difficult aspects such as fan kicks, which require more flexibility than I currently have, and then a major back bend off the floor to a standing position. I got through it fairly well but was a bit surprised when I was asked to stay and sing.

I had the opportunity to use the technique that I've begun to develop in Paul's class and although I was still a little nervous I gave a good performance. Barry asked me to sing it again with more volume so I did, and he and the others at the table nodded their heads in agreement.

I was given some sides and then went back to the waiting room to read them over and prepare. I had the opportunity to practice with a guy who refreshed my memory on who the characters were in the scene (I wasn't as prepared as I could have been!) and then sat and waited while the others finished singing. The readings went pretty well and I had the chance to read the roles of Ren and Willard several times. Finally they had a few of us stay and dance one more time and again I did pretty well.

Afterward I was getting my stuff together in the waiting room and talking to Katherine on the phone when the producer asked me back in to read some more. This time I did cold readings of Wes Warnicker and the cop and finally was seen for the roles I originally thought I was right for. Barry seemed pleased with the way I read and then I left. What a day of auditions!

*November 12, Wednesday.*
A recent e-mail responding to New Trier senior Peter Hart:

> *Peter,*
> *Nice to hear from you. Sorry for the delayed response, it's been a busy week. Things are going well. I had some recent success at an audition for* Footloose *for a theatre up in Westchester. I had several callbacks and I was still left at the end and reading for some adult roles in the show. I don't think I'll get it but that's OK. It's about the process, and a callback helps a lot! If I were to get it I would get my Equity card through the show, which would be great.*
>
> *We go into the studio tomorrow to start creating a CD for* The Kid Who Played the Palace. *I'm in only two numbers but it should be fun. There will be staged readings of the show starting in January. It's slow going but interesting. The Bravo thing is actually about one of the actors in the show. The premise of the show is they're following around people from different walks of life and giving the viewer an inside look at what it's like to be an: actor, photographer, Wall Street exec, etc. The actor happens to be in* The Kid Who Played the Palace *so they filmed several rehearsals as part of his portion of the show. If I'm in it, it would be just as a scene partner as we sing through stuff. Nothing fancy. The show apparently doesn't air until spring!*

*November 16, Sunday.*
What follows is a recent e-mail sent out to everyone on my e-mail list:

> *Hello All,*
> *First mass e-mail in a long time. Please forgive as usual. Some recent good news. About a week and a half ago I had a long day of auditioning that started with a dance call for a production of* Pippin *followed by another dance call for* Footloose. *I felt good about the*

Pippin *call but no callback. The choreography was very Fosse-esque and fun to do but I can honestly say I didn't completely ace it.*

*I got through the* Footloose *dance call ('80s disco and country) and with all the youth in the room I fully expected to be cut, but to my surprise received a callback. I was asked to sing and after my sixteen bars of "Lost in the Wilderness" they gave me sides (dialogue from the show) to study. I practiced a bit with another guy and after about an hour of sitting around I went in and read for two different youth parts. At this point, of the about one hundred nonunion male actors who started the afternoon (the morning was filled with union guys) there were about ten left: me and nine twenty-somethings. They asked us all to repeat the dance again and then finally let us go. As everyone left I called Katherine from the waiting room and the producer called me in to read yet again. This time, I read for some of the adult roles and then they released me.*

*I got called a couple of days ago and was cast in the show. I'll be playing some supporting adult roles and will be in the ensemble. The production is being done at Westchester Broadway Theatre in Elmsford, New York, which is just outside the city. It's a very reputable theatre on the same par with perhaps the Marriott Lincolnshire. The best part about being cast is that the contract will offer me the opportunity to join the actors union in the last two weeks of the run. I will now be getting my Equity card!*

*I must also admit that I'm still not fully recovered from the day of dance. I pulled some muscle in my back and I'm still suffering.*

*I've been taking a musical theatre audition class, which has been incredibly helpful, and have begun to take voice lessons with a teacher here in the city. When my back fully heals I will resume taking class at Dance Space Center.*

*November 18, Tuesday.*

I had my third class with Paul Harman yesterday and I'm starting to feel as though I have a handle on the technique. It helps to have some items of the audition under my own control. Paul has really enlightened me and I look forward to doing more auditions in the future to see how I do. Since the audition where I hurt my back, however, I'm having a hard time standing for more than five to ten minutes. Paul doesn't mind that I have to sit down now and then.

*November 21, Friday.*

Some recent updates.

Katherine had an agent call for *Mamma Mia* a week ago and it went very well, but doing so doesn't mean much. She's really only after leading, more mature type roles so there's not very much out there. She was up for Fastrada for the Emelin dinner theatre production of *Pippin* I mentioned earlier and also did really well, but it was apparent that the theatre did most of its hiring from within its small family of regulars. Hopefully, something will pop for her soon. She deserves it!

*Footloose* starts rehearsal on February 2 and opens on the 11th. It will run until May 1 so it's a nice long run. I don't get my card until the last two weeks. The contract stipulates a three-week out so I obviously wouldn't leave unless I had a great offer that offered me my card outright. I'm really thrilled because getting my card was something I always wanted and one of my major goals.

I just spent the last two days in a recording studio with *The Kid Who Played the Palace*. Peter Sklar, the guy who conceived the show and wrote the music, is trying to get the show moving forward. The CD will go out to prospective producers and then there will be some staged readings in January. I don't know if I'll still be with it if and when it goes to production. I'll say this: It's a lovely score and a compelling story. It certainly has potential and is a showcase for teenagers.

I'm still struggling with my lower back and then woke up this morning with another area, between my shoulder blades, all seized up. I'm not doing well! I need to get back to my cardio workouts because the muscles that are freaked out are muscles of endurance and they need a lot of circulation. Once I get back to the cross-trainer I think I'll be OK.

*November 26, Wednesday.*
I finally went to a doctor today for my back. I can't put my pants on without an extreme amount of pain and even walking is difficult. The doctor, who came highly recommended to me from Anne-Rene Lawton, my dance teacher, came in to do some initial analysis and then forgot about me. I waited at least a half-hour and it wasn't until a nurse came into clean up at the end of the day that they realized I was still there. He didn't apologize but instead tried to cover for himself and it really angered me. The most important thing, though, was for me to get a referral for therapy, and I got a prescription from him for that purpose.

I'm going to the Macy's Thanksgiving Day Parade tomorrow. Paul and his partner Stephen live three doors away from Central Park West (part of the parade route). I'll hang out with Stephen and then walk over. I'm not a big parade fan, but since we're here....

*November 27, Thursday.*
This morning I went to the Macy's parade and had a good time. I had trouble getting through the crowd on my way to Stephen's apartment on Seventy-fourth Street and they were already on their way down to the parade. They took ladders into the street and set them up to see over the crowd. It worked pretty well and I was able to see a lot. Tim Schultheis was there with a co-worker and the co-worker's son. The parade wasn't the most exciting thing I've ever seen, and being closer would have made it a little more interesting, but now I can say I've seen this famous parade.

# December

*December 4, Thursday.*

We returned last night from La Jolla, California, where we spent the past five days visiting Katherine's family, including her ninety-five-year-old grandmother, and having another Thanksgiving dinner. Although the weather was a tad on the chilly side, it was great to get away from the city.

*December 11, Thursday.*

Audition #16. I had an audition today for the Encores series (this season's shows are *Can-Can, Pardon My English,* and *Bye Bye Birdie*) at City Center at Ripley Grier Studios. It was the first audition that was intended only for Equity members that I crashed. To my dismay, they had a list for nonunion people! Had I known that they did this, I would have been going to union calls six months ago. This was the best audition I've had since I've come to New York! I sang really well ("I Won't Send Roses") and I owe it all to Paul's class. I was prepared with the song, was able to tune out every other distraction, and pursued the goal I had given myself for that performance. Jack Viertel, the artistic director, and Kathleen Marshall, the resident director, were at the table and they were very complimentary. I think I am a perfect type for the Shriner guys in *Birdie.*

*December 14, Sunday.*

Audition #17. I auditioned yesterday for *Bare: A Pop Opera* and really had a good time. This was another Equity audition where I was allowed to be seen. I was so ancient in comparison with the rest of the actors waiting to sing and I felt like a parent waiting to see a concert of Christina Aguilera with all of her wannabes. The show did require a man in his thirties or early forties for the role of the priest, and when Dave Clemmons, the casting director, asked what I was going to sing, he was relieved when I said "The Mason" from *Working.* He said, "Ah, finally a real song," for he and his colleague (perhaps the composer Damon Intrabartolo) had been hearing a lot of awful pop stuff all day long. The accompanist was fantastic and really supportive. She's a very popular Asian woman who is known in the community, but I can't remember her name at the moment. I sang pretty well and did pretty much what I set out to do, but it's a very challenging song that I need to work on more.

*December 16, Tuesday.*

Audition #18. I went to a chorus call today for *Gypsy* at Chelsea Studios and sang for Jim Carnahan, the casting director. I sang a new version of "Come Back to Me" that Ken Lundy had rearranged for me, and I had a brief memory slip. I've been singing a different version of it since 1987 and didn't really give myself enough time with the new version to make it work the way I wanted it. The mistake was not very noticeable and the accompanist actually took the blame, apologizing as he gave my book back to me. An OK audition but actually quite forgettable.

*December 17, Wednesday.*

I went today for my back consultation/evaluation at the Hospital for Joint Diseases. I'm in bad shape but the problem isn't so acute anymore. The therapist, Bliss, showed me some exercises to start developing muscles that I hadn't even known existed. Kegel exercises train the deep girdle muscles of the abdomen and back. If these muscles are working better, my back will heal more quickly. I will start with a different therapist on Monday.

*December 19, Friday.*

Audition #19. Yesterday I attended an "Equity male ensemble dancers who sing" call for *Chicago*. I finally had the opportunity to audition for this show! I was not in quite good enough shape to do well at this audition—because of my still-ailing back, I haven't been able to attend enough dance classes—but I gave it an earnest try. I was quite surprised to have to learn a ballet combination because the show is strictly Fosse-style jazz. I got a little panicked with so many superb dancers in the room who could execute the ballet moves with ease. I tried too hard and was barely mediocre when it came time to perform the combination. I did OK at the jazz but many were far better. Apparently, the same combination from the show is used for every six-month required call, and so many were very prepared. Gary Chryst, who used to dance with Joffrey Ballet and was a co-choreographer with Anne Reinking on the show, teamed up with the dance captain to run the audition. They were fun to work with and added a lot of laughter and joy to the process. It still didn't change the fact that it was an intense audition for a Broadway show, however. Needless to say, they kept only a few to sing and let the rest of us go. I think I will try again in six months.

The previous four auditions were all union calls and I was allowed to participate in every one of them. Considering that I won't receive my Equity card until late April, I will continue to attend these Equity calls. I also don't think I will ever attend another audition for a nonunion show!

*December 22, Monday*

I had my first physical therapy session today with Emelie. I was a bit worried because she seemed so young, but after a short time I could sense that she really knew what she was doing. She worked with me quite a while stretching certain parts of my back and legs and giving me exercises to do. I must admit my back already feels a little better.

*December 24, Wednesday.*

Another session today with Emelie and again I'm feeling better. She's very good, and it's apparent in the clinic that the other therapists have a lot of respect for her knowledge of the back. She likes me because I can immediately assimilate the exercises she gives me. She says sometimes it takes people weeks to understand what she wants them to do. I'm so thankful that I'm on the road to recovery.

*December 25, Thursday.*

Christmas in NYC. Katherine and I had a very special and quiet Christmas in New York City. Since the budget was small we opted for good food and a few gifts and had a lovely evening to ourselves. We allowed ourselves to have some downtime and enjoyed each other's company for forty-eight hours.

*December 31, Wednesday.*

My brother Richard, his wife, Sue, and their children—Valerie, eighteen, Emily, fifteen, and Taylor, twelve—visited us from Sussex, Wisconsin, over the past four days. It was fun having them because they were very gung-ho on the city. They'd get up early and head out and we'd end up meeting them somewhere later in the day for dinner before they tackled another sight or show. Although we had seven in our two-bedroom, one-bath place, it was very easy. They did a lot of bus tours and saw several shows. We went down to see Ground Zero, which had a profound effect on us all. We'll always remember their visit.

## January 2004

*January 3, 2004, Saturday.*

We've been in NYC for exactly six months and it has been an incredible experience so far. It took a long time for me to slow down from my teacher pace and settle into a routine here. I've done nineteen auditions thus far but I am growing more selective with that process. Our apartment feels like home and, although it is a little removed from Times Square and the places where we do a lot of our business, it is nice to use that separation to disconnect from it all. Lance is fully at home in the apartment as well. He loves the large windowsills because he can lie down and sleep in the sun. He's starting to show his age and has a significant limp. I think he has arthritis in one of his rear hips. I can relate.

*January 16, Friday.*

Audition #20. I sat and waited yesterday to audition for a chorus call for *The Producers*. I got there at 12:30 in order to sign up on the non-Equity list and then proceeded to wait for four hours before I finally had to leave for a physical therapy appointment. Very disappointing, but needless to say there was a very high chance that I wouldn't have ever gotten in because of the huge list of union people waiting to sing. I'm still going to count it as an audition!

*January 19, Monday.*

I finished up today with Paul Harman's class. I have one unscheduled session remaining so I hope to get that in sometime after the show goes up. I must say it was the best $360 I ever spent. I have so many tools now to craft a song for an audition and I can use parts of this technique to help students be a little more comfortable with the audition process.

The best part is controlling how the beginning of my performance starts rather than being at the mercy of the accompanist. It feels good to have control over the flow of my audition, to wrest back some of the power from the people at the table.

*January 23, Friday.*
We saw *Taboo* last night after one of Katherine's classmates in Paul Harman's class (we were in different sessions) handed her two $100 tickets for free. We wouldn't have seen this show otherwise but it was an interesting piece. The show was based on the life of Boy George and the people in his life in the punk dance club world of London in the early eighties. A very interesting premise with a multitalented cast but a mediocre score and uneven script. The show had some serious flaws but we enjoyed the talent. Boy George, who now goes by the name George O'Dowd, played Leigh Bowery, a famous performance artist in 1980s London who died from AIDS in 1994. Although Bowery had an interesting character and life, O'Dowd's portrayal was weak, in my eyes. This was due to both predictable, one-dimensional writing and O'Dowd's playing himself rather than building a believable character. The guy who played the young George was wonderful and there were other great performances, but I found myself not caring about the characters and that's always a bad sign!

*January 25, Sunday.*
Body report: Well, I have been in New York City for six and a half months and can honestly say that I am finally in excellent shape.

The Gym: My gym-type workouts have slowly progressed to the point where I do twenty vigorous minutes on a cross trainer for cardiovascular health followed by about ten minutes of abdominal work and stretching. After that I lift weights, alternating each workout on either my upper or lower body. I have not achieved my personal best in many exercise categories but I have in many others. I like to work primarily with free weights and focus almost exclusively with dumbbells. I find that this is the most beneficial for me because it requires core strength to balance separate weights and strengthens each side of my body more evenly. I am to the point now where I can bench- and incline-press thirty-five-pound dumbbells and would like to work my way up to fifty. (My personal best was sixty-pound dumbbells when I was twenty-eight years old. This is no longer a realistic goal.) I have struggled consistently with tendinitis in both shoulders, which has slowed me down. I've managed to work through it, however—a major victory. My lower-body workouts reach new heights each day because I have never focused for this length of time on that part of my body. I didn't even start lower-body workouts until about three years ago because dance had always taken care of that aspect.

Dance Class: I have recently upped my trips to class to twice a week. I have noticed a huge difference in my leg and core strength and feel that I have a much greater understanding about dance and my body than ever before. When I was in my early twenties, I studied intensely at Gus Giordano's in Evanston, trying to make up for the lack of training I'd had at that point in my career. I used to take up to ten classes a week, thinking that if I just went a lot I would soak it all up. I learned a lot but now I find that a couple of highly focused classes are enough to get the job done. I am currently studying Simonson Technique—a very organic form of modern jazz—at Dance Space Center and find it to be exactly what my body can handle. Ballet would be too demanding and tap isn't something I particularly care to develop at this point in my life. (I tapped in *42nd Street* and *Me and My Girl* already, two of the most demanding and popular tap shows in Broadway history, and that was enough.) Simonson is demanding but I can manage the class with the least amount of stress to my body.

The Bod: In the last dance class I took (last Thursday) I reinjured my left hamstring for the umpty-umpth time and it's taking time to heal. This injury goes all the way back to high school when I overstretched this muscle in order to achieve the splits for gymnastic competition. Since then it has been prone to injury. Shoulders are a bit creaky and clicky but nothing too painful. In general I'm OK and I think I'll be in good shape when *Footloose* starts in a week.

# February

*February 2, Monday.*
We had our first rehearsal today for *Footloose* and I had an enjoyable and interesting time. Of course there were the usual introductions and awkwardness of not knowing people at first. It seemed, however, that I was one of the only people who basically knew nobody; everyone else seemed to be greeting their long-lost friends.

We sang first and learned a lot of the material for the show, and then we spent the afternoon working on different country waltz steps with Barry McNabb and the assistant Amber Stone. It was a lot of fun and doable for me, but after the day's worth of exercise, I was feeling it.

*February 3, Tuesday.*
We continued with the country section of the show today, finishing the waltz sections and then working on "Let's Hear It for the Boy." Toby Foster is playing Rusty and she's got a great voice for the song. She's a triple threat and seems equally comfortable in all realms: strong singer, dancer, actor. My Cowboy Bob character has a lot to do with her in this scene so she and I are getting to know each other quite well. Other than Chris DeAngelis from my Great America days (1987), I know no one in this cast.

*February 9, Monday.*
I haven't written much about the rehearsal process because I have been so exhausted from the physical and mental strain of learning new material. However, today we had a daylight day off so I recuperated a little. This evening we're in the space at Westchester

Broadway Theatre for the first time. I was impressed with the size of the place. It's very big and a tremendous amount of people were there helping load in the show. It should be a nice production.

The week since my last journal entry has been frantic and a little scary. We have such a short time to get it all together and just yesterday we did a run-through of the show for the first time. Although space was very limited in the studio, it went well and I had the chance to see all of the great talent in the show. Shonn Wiley, who plays Ren, is such a natural, and it's a pleasure to watch him work. He's got a great voice for musical theatre and I think he will play Ren well. Joe Dellger, who's playing Shaw Moore, is originally from Wisconsin and was in a group that I was in called The Kids From Wisconsin. I hope we have a chance to exchange some stories about that experience sometime. He's fabulous in this role; he has an excellent voice and is a strong actor. He's playing opposite a Broadway veteran, Joy Franz, who's done ten B'Way shows. It's fun to work with the consummate professional.

I'm fortunate in that I have a consistent ride to the theatre in a car directly from my neighborhood. Ed Romanoff, who plays the coach as well as other supporting characters, lives a few blocks from me, and he's offered me a seat in his car, which is awesome. I think Shonn will also ride along, so we'll have a full car but it won't be terribly packed. It's such a luxury to have this opportunity and not have to ride in the van! It should be interesting to be part of this threesome, as both of them are veterans of the business.

We had our first rehearsal with the orchestra today. I can't believe we are doing a preview of this show for an audience in two days.

*February 19, Thursday.*
*Footloose* had its official opening last night and although the last week has been rough, the opening went really well. There was a party afterward and it was exciting to be a part of a show again. Katherine and our friend Eric Kincaid came and met the cast members that I've gotten to know. It was a highly festive atmosphere and I didn't want to leave!

*February 24, Tuesday.*
Audition #21. I went to an audition yesterday for a new Goodspeed Opera production called *All Shook Up*. It's slated to run for six weeks in Connecticut in May-June, two months in Chicago in December-January 2005 and then have a Broadway opening sometime in summer of 2005. It features the songs of Elvis Presley and is loosely based on Shakespeare's *A Midsummer Night's Dream* and *Twelfth Night*. The accompanist, a man in his early 40s, was rude to me and although I felt I was well prepared, I wasn't anticipating attitude from my usual ally. I was distracted and didn't do as well as I had hoped with the classic "Splish Splash," and he didn't play as well as he should have.

(My friend Paul Castree ended up being cast in this production and performed in the May-June Goodspeed slot, a month in Chicago, and then a four-month Broadway run.)

# March

*March 3, Wednesday.*

Audition #22. Auditions were held today for a new production of *Chitty Chitty Bang Bang* and I attended. It was an EPA so I had a full two minutes to sing. The show doesn't go up for over a year so this had a significant influence on why I had to wait only for an hour. They are having three separate calls over the next two months and this one was the first of the three. People often don't bother with the first one, preferring to wait until later for obvious reasons (more prep time, closer to the start date of the show, etc.). I sang the full selection of "Come With Me" from *Boys From Syracuse* and did alright. I got a little tight on the upper notes and that is the opposite of what I need to be doing. This is a tough song to sing when that happens because it's so high at the end. I didn't much care about the result since the show is so far away and not anything I could ever consider.

*March 8, Monday.*

Audition #23. I went to an EPA today for Cohoe Music Hall's production of *Mame*. It looked like a good show for me, a good, strong singer who moves well and who could play supporting roles. Alas, they decided after I'd waited two hours that they weren't going to see any nonunion actors; they had already filled a quota for employing nonunion for the season. If they knew this, wouldn't it have been courteous to tell the nonunion people they wouldn't be seen before they waited for two hours?

We went to see *Little Shop of Horrors* on Broadway last night. The opening of the show was fantastic. The trio was really the best that you could imagine this threesome to be. They were flawless musicians with powerful voices but were also superb actors embracing the attitude of the roles. The thing that made it all the more impressive was that one of the three was the understudy. Their harmonies were perfectly blended and you would have never known which of the three was not normally a part of this group.

The bass who was the voice of Audrey II had a rare quality that you don't often hear. There was such depth to his voice and he was also a fine musician. We had the chance to see the actor in the musical number "Skid Row" when he pulled a blanket off his head to sing, "then you go…" It was a clever bit of shtick that worked beautifully.

*March 10, Wednesday.*

Audition #24. Paper Mill Playhouse held auditions today for its production of *Guys and Dolls* at Chelsea Studios. The non-Equity male singers audition started at two (women were in the morning) and so I arrived about an hour early to sign up. An hour in advance put me 128th on the list! The place was absolutely packed so I left and sat at Starbucks for about an hour reading the paper. When I got back to the studio around 2:30, they were on number 35, so I found a place to sit in the front room and started reading my current book (the fourth Harry Potter). I sat for about an hour and a half. Then, as it finally started getting close to the time I would sing, I ran downstairs to the sidewalk and hummed a little to get my voice warmed up again. Finally, about 4:20, I was put in the line. Just before I was to go into the room I was informed that they wanted only eight bars (the notice said "brief traditional musical theatre song," which usually means sixteen bars). I quickly cut an already butchered version of "Come Back to Me" down to eight bars in about thirty seconds and then, in a state of semi-panic, proceeded into the audition room. I was not very focused and allowed my anger to prevent me from giving a good performance. They said thank you and I left.

This was probably the most frustrating audition I've had since being here. It was sort of the final straw on the camel's back in terms of how I feel about pursuing the business any further. First of all the fact that 150 nonunion actors showed up to audition for parts that probably only one or two would get brought home to me the dire despair of working in the business. All for a job that would pay $450 a week at best, not even enough to pay your rent in NYC. Secondly, the fact that I had to sit for so long a time and then be expected to perform brilliantly with eight bars of music seems idiotic to me. I know that's the business, but no matter what I try, my voice just doesn't work that way. I need to be warmed up. I also think the directors who ask for eight bars are, in general, lazy. Most directors will call people in to be typed first and then give the people they kept an opportunity to perform at least sixteen bars of music. Although it seems a tad brutal, it actually saves time for all involved and gives people a legitimate shot. Someone who asks for eight bars is basically saying, "I really don't have much interest in you, but if you can blow me away in eight bars I might consider you." I've had it!

*March 11, Thursday.*
Syrus Nemat-Nasser, Katherine's brother, is here visiting for a week. He's rescued our computer, which had been rendered practically unusable because of viruses and spyware. He completely wiped our hard drive clean and then reinstalled our operating system with all of the updates that we had neglected to install (some forty-two!). After more fine-tuning, he deleted the programs we wouldn't need and installed an antivirus and a firewall. Although it's an old computer, it is now running beautifully.

*March 17, Wednesday.*
Audition #25. Today I went to an audition for a production of *Ragtime* that is being produced by Actors Company at the Fulton. There's not much to say about this audition. There was a large group of people at the table and they were all very friendly. I sang "Sometimes a Day Goes By," which, it turns out, was not enough of a piece to sing for a show like *Ragtime*. My original thinking was that I should let them hear me singing a

song that I'm comfortable with and that shows off my voice in its best light, but I should have picked something a bit more dramatic. I'm still learning.

# April

*April 5, Monday.*

Audition #26. I went to an EPA today for a new Broadway production of *Dracula*. They were kind enough to see nonunion people at this EPA and surprisingly not that many people were there. The show was written by Frank Wildhorn, who also wrote *Jekyll and Hyde* and *The Scarlet Pimpernel*. They asked for a song that was dramatic and dark by nature so I sang the only song I have that's close to that, "Words He Doesn't Say." Man, I wish I had sung better. It was an average performance but it was an opportunity for me to make a good impression on Dave Clemmons, the casting director. Several others from *Footloose* are auditioning for this show. It will be interesting to see how they do. (Shonn Wiley, who played Ren in *Footloose*, ended up being cast as a lead in this production.)

*April 13, Tuesday.*

During a lesson today, Judith offered Katherine and me a European tour of an Andrew Lloyd Webber concert/revue. We'd rehearse in NY for a week, fly to Switzerland to rehearse for another week, and then proceed to Italy for a three-week tour. It took us quite by surprise, but it's all very exciting. The contract will cover all travel and lodging expenses plus one meal a day and pay $400 a week for two weeks of rehearsal and 500 euros a week ($615) for the three-week run. Lots to consider with regard to going back to New Trier, the move, and the cat. However, it just goes to show how important connections are!

*April 14, Wednesday.*

My brother Dick and his family (minus my niece Valerie, who had school conflicts) have been staying with us over the past four days. Once again they attacked the city but with a more laser-like fashion this time around. They came up from Manhattan by train to Westchester to see the show. I didn't have as much free time because of my commitments with the show but still managed to see them quite a bit.

Two days ago, on the 12th, Katherine and I went to opening day of the Mets with Paul and Stephen at Shea. It was a cold, rainy, miserable day but we had fun anyway. The Mets won the game but almost blew a ten-run lead toward the end.

*April 21, Wednesday.*

I signed my union contract today! It turned out to be a very special occasion. WBT took the time and made the effort to make the event a special one for us by providing champagne and toasting the achievement. Lisa Tiso (producer/company manager), David Cunningham (producer/production manager), and John McNamara (production stage manager) were on hand to drink with Jarod Stein, Robin Wilner, and me.

*April 22, Thursday.*

My mother, Marilyn; my brother Andrew; his wife, Donna; and two of their sons, Colin, thirteen, and Ethan, eighteen months, arrived today from Wisconsin for an NYC visit. They'll be staying with us until Sunday and will do some exploring on their first visit to the city. Colin is a bit upset that he had to miss a seventh-grade dance, but I think he'll be OK after he sees a little of the city.

*April 23, Friday.*

Today Andy and I rented a car and took the family sightseeing. We passed the passenger piers at Forty-second Street on the way downtown and saw the new Queen Mary 2, the largest passenger vessel afloat. It dwarfed the pier itself and was surrounded by security.

Our main destination was Ground Zero. It was my second time so I drove around the area to avoid having to park the car, and the rest of them had a chance to really take it all in. I could tell that it had a profound effect on them, but their spirits remained high as the day continued.

After Ground Zero we headed uptown to the Upper West Side and found a nice but expensive restaurant to have lunch. As we were trying to find a place to park I showed them the Dakota, where John Lennon was living when he was killed. I walk by it at least once a week and don't think twice now, but I do remember the first time I saw it. It gives a little better perception of a life and event that were so very important to us.

In the evening I drove everyone up to the theatre so they could attend *Footloose*. They had poor seats but I was able to arrange for them to move just prior to showtime. They seemed to like the show and were happy to see me perform one last time.

*April 24, Saturday.*

My mom and I saw *42nd Street* today. Had decent seats about twenty-five rows back in the center of the orchestra section. An old friend from Opryland, David Elder, has been playing Billy Lawlor in the show since it opened three years ago and I'd hoped to have the chance to talk to him after the show. However, he wasn't on for the matinee, which was a little disappointing. The show was first-rate. Good quality musical theatre entertainment. I didn't realize how big the cast would be. When I performed in *42nd Street* on the Norway, we had a total of eighteen cast members. This production had fifty-five in it with thirty-six just in the ensemble. Of course this makes for spectacular production numbers. The set on this enormous stage was fantastic. The choreography, for all practical purposes, was the same as the original.

*April 26, Monday.*

After Sunday brunch yesterday at 107 West, one of our favorite restaurants in our neighborhood, I went to work and the family went back to Wisconsin. I think Colin ended up having a great time!

*April 27, Tuesday.*

Continued work on voice range in my lesson today. Also, I began to prepare for the Euro tour by singing "Wilkommen" from Cabaret. Judith really likes my voice for this song. Also sang Lt. Cable's "Younger than Springtime," "When the Children Are Asleep," and "I Won't Send Roses." The voice was in a great spot today.

*April 29, Thursday.*

This morning we talked with Leo Passov (the man whose apartment we are subletting) about the possibility of extending our sublet for a month in order to accommodate the tour to Italy in July and August, and he agreed. Now we will be able to keep Lance in the same space and he'll hopefully have people here to sit for him. This would be the optimal setting for us because we can still be here when we rehearse in July and then we'll be gone only a month. Lance can stay in his comfortable surroundings and when we get back it will be just a short trip for him back to the Evanston townhouse.

I have five shows left of *Footloose* and I am ready for it to be over and to move on to the next phase of my life. I've enjoyed the experience and am grateful for the opportunity to obtain union status. It was good to get back into performing again and to remember what it's like to go to work every day on a show.

I must admit I haven't been too faithful in maintaining my journal during this time. The show took the energy and desire right out of me. Other than what turned out to be a familiar grind of a show, there hasn't been much to write about. But what seems familiar to me may be unfamiliar to some people who will read this diary, so here's a little look at what it's like to be in a professional show.

When students do shows in school, the rehearsal process is generally six to eight weeks long, followed by three to eight performances. Summer stock productions rehearse for two weeks and then there is usually a weeklong run of eight performances. These experiences are brief in nature and the show is exciting during its run. However, when an actor works in regional, touring, or Broadway shows, the show runs for a much longer period of time. For regional productions, shows typically run for three months. National tours can have an open-ended run; it isn't unusual for an actor to work anywhere from a year to five years if the show is a blockbuster. The same applies to Broadway productions. A long run of a show is an actor's dream because it is the elusive steady work uncommon in show business. Many actors will stay with an open-ended run for a year or two and then move on as they grow tired of repeating the same role eight times a week. Others find a way to keep it fresh and stay with a production for years. Marlene Danielle was in the original company of *Cats* on Broadway and was still in it when the show closed eighteen years later.

The longest I stayed with a show was one year with *Cats* in Zurich, Switzerland. I was able to do this because I played three different roles. I tended to grow tired of playing the same part after a while. I found the creative aspect of mounting the production the most exciting and rewarding. The run of the show grew tiresome, especially if the show was physically exhausting like *Cats* or the Opryland shows I performed in. For me it was always a double-edged sword: glad to be working consistently but bored with the daily repetitive routine.

Most union contracts are for eight shows a week with one or two days off. A typical schedule might be as follows: Tuesday evening show, Wednesday matinee and evening shows, Thursday and Friday evening shows, Saturday matinee and evening shows, Sunday matinee (or evening) show, and then Monday off. Some schedules will have two shows on Sunday in lieu of the Tuesday performance and have both Monday and Tuesday off. Most actors refer to Monday (and Tuesday) as "the weekend." I always found the schedule to be similar to a second-shift kind of job. Rise late in the morning, eat a late breakfast (10:30 a.m. or so), a late lunch (in the late afternoon), and then go to the theatre around 6:00 p.m. There I would prepare for the show with physical and vocal warm-up, preset my costumes, and apply makeup; then the show would begin at 8 p.m. After the show finished, usually around 10:30 p.m., I was always wound up and hungry so I would have dinner around 11:00 p.m. and get to bed around 1 or 2 a.m. Then, I'd rise at 10 a.m. and do it all again!

*April 30, Friday.*
I spent a lot of time running errands today and feel good about getting things done. I went to the Equity office to get my card only to discover that they wouldn't take a credit card! How very stupid and archaic of them. All of the paperwork is finished, however, and all I have to do is return to the office and pay the $400 down payment. I will then have several years to pay the remaining balance for the $1,100 membership fee.

I also applied to renew my passport, which had plenty of challenges not worthy of writing about. The only advice I have at this point is that if you are a performer and would ever consider working abroad—where there is a lot of work, by the way—get a passport now. In case you are offered a contract that requires you to leave quickly you will save yourself upwards of several hundred dollars in "rush" fees. Just get the passport <u>now</u>. Fortunately, Katherine and I have plenty of time to have them done at the normal fee of $85 apiece. (By 2011, the fees had gone up to $110 for renewal and an extra $25 acceptance fee for a first-time passport.)

After that I went to the gym and then home to rest before the Friday evening show. Tomorrow is the last day of *Footloose*.

## May

*May 2, Sunday.*
*Footloose* closed last night and I am drained from the last performance's emotional high. It was an intense experience, and because I had been looking forward to the end of the contract, I didn't expect to be at all emotional. I guess that no matter the experience,

when a portion of your life ends there is inevitable reflection and a sense of joy mixed with loss. The party afterward was festive and the theatre provided an open bar for the cast, crew, and production team. I drank red wine and enjoyed myself immensely! I had a good conversation with the director, Barry McNabb, who thanked me for bringing my talent and professionalism to the show. He had worked with Katherine years before and spoke highly and fondly of her also. I was very happy that I'd represented myself well in this situation, because you never know when another opportunity will present itself. The show-business world is incredibly small.

I'll miss the people the most. I really grew to like my fellow cast members, even though I felt I didn't have much in common with most of them. I became good friends with Joe Dellger, from Plymouth, Wisconsin, and will probably continue to stay in touch with him. He and I have golf plans for later in the summer. Toward the end of the run I also found friendship with some other Midwestern types who joined in a euchre game. Shonn Wiley, Jarod Stein, Blake Ginther, Joe, and I had some intense card battles as the show drew to a close. I wish we'd thought of that earlier in the run!

*May 3, Monday.*
After paying the initial minimum of $400, I secured my Equity card! The cost is now $1,100 to join the union. When Katherine joined in 1981, it was $300! I have my official temporary card and it's already in my wallet. Hopefully, I'll be able to use it a few times for auditions before I leave NYC.

*May 4, Tuesday.*
We leave tomorrow for Florida to visit Katherine's dad. It's been a long time since we've been out of the city, Thanksgiving in fact, and it will be good to get some perspective. We'll be there for a week and play some golf. The only drawback is that I will miss an audition for *Mamma Mia* while we're gone. I would actually be very right for a dad cover/ensemble in that show. (Because the show has three dad roles, three male members of the ensemble learn one role each and are ready to cover for that dad in case of illness or injury.) Oh well.

*May 13, Thursday.*
We left Florida yesterday and had a frustrating day of travel. Because of inclement weather in NY, our flight to LaGuardia was delayed twice, then finally canceled! We ended up flying into JFK at 1:30 this morning, six and a half hours after we were originally supposed to arrive. Ahhh!

Our trip was great. We played three rounds of golf, visited the Golf Hall of Fame outside St. Augustine, did some much-needed shopping at Target (there is no Target in NYC), and hung around a lot with Katherine's dad, John, and his girlfriend, Barbara. It was nice to get away and feel some real heat after a very long winter.

*May 15, Saturday.*

Today I decided late in the morning to go to the gym for the second time in two days after an eleven-day layoff. As I was crossing Central Park West at Sixty-third Street I crossed paths with John Lithgow, who was on his way to the park with his dog. He seemed tall and ordinary with a baseball cap on and a mutty dog on a leash. It just goes to show that NYC is the best place in the world for stars to reside because they blend right into the mainstream.

I also plan to return to dance class starting on Sunday. It's been almost three and a half months since I last took class. I'll be rusty but I'm very excited about it. I really enjoy it. I have one final goal before I return to Evanston and that's to audition one more time for *Chicago* and get called back to sing. If I can do that, I'll know that I danced well.

*May 18, Tuesday.*

I had a voice lesson today after a three-week layoff. I was a bit rusty and took more time to find the groove, but I did get there for the most part. After about forty minutes of vocalizing, we started working on "Master of the House" and Judith helped me with a different placement for the piece. It was a more nasal placement to help me create an obnoxious sound but to stay off my cords. I was able to do it but then struggled a little going back to the other sound for "Wilkommen." Ah, the challenges of my singing.

I'm looking forward to the tour after talking with Judith. She's having us over to her house for cocktails in a week or so for the cast to meet each other and discuss the trip. We will also have a vocal rehearsal on June 13 to learn the music so we can come to the first staging rehearsal on July 9 with the music learned.

*May 29, Saturday.*

I have an audition for *Chicago* in less than a week. It's a required six-month chorus call so they are definitely not casting out of this audition, but if I could just impress the people at the table enough for a callback to sing, I will consider it a success and another goal achieved. I am trying to remember the two dance combinations that were used last December, one ballet and one directly from the opening of the show.

Over the past few days my voice has started to feel really good. I have a lesson on Tuesday and I hope I can build on what I've achieved. I also want to be in good shape for the audition in case I am asked to sing.

# June

*June 2, Wednesday.*

I had a full day yesterday, all activities primarily aimed to help with preparation for my audition for *Chicago* on Friday. I dropped off an old pair of white jazz shoes at the shoe repair shop to have them dyed black and cleaned up. I then went down for a haircut and then to the Equity office to sign up for *Chicago*. This, by the way, was the first time

I was able to sign up for an audition because of my new Equity status. I was also able to use the lounge and the bathroom. Ah, such simple pleasures. I proceeded to the gym for a lower-body workout and then spent a little time in the aerobics room working on the two dance combinations that I remember from the last audition.

After my workout I had a lesson and it went very well. Although I was singing over a lot of allergy-related problems, I accomplished a lot. The upper range continues to develop and I am more consistently singing with more space, volume, color, and depth than ever before. Judith has been great for me, as has having a whole year away from the vocal strain of teaching. We worked on the two songs I want to have ready for the audition, and then we worked on the songs I will sing in the show. It all went well.

Today my back is feeling very tight so I think I will have to lie low for most of the day. I did go down and pick up my shoes and they turned out beautifully. I'm spending a lot of time right now compiling the information I collected in the actor survey and preparing to finish the sabbatical project. I will finish the journal on June 30, the one-year mark.

*June 5, Saturday.*
Audition #27. I auditioned yesterday for *Chicago* and I was cut after the first round of dancing. I felt very prepared for the audition, having remembered a majority of both combinations (Fosse and ballet) from six months earlier. My weakness came in the improv sections of the Fosse, where I truly stumbled. I had thought of some movement but wasn't able to execute at the tempo that they set so I looked a little frantic. The Fosse I executed very well and although I was at the downstage center of the three in my group, and thus exposed without being able to see anyone in my peripheral vision, I was confident in the presentation. I also felt good about the fact that I was the only guy who looked like me at the audition. My height, light hair and eyes, and lean, cut look were in contrast to the majority of the dancers who were dark, short, and bulky. I guess they wanted the latter!

I was disappointed with my audition and lamented afterward that I couldn't do more with the improv in the moment. In this way only do I feel I choked. It was the first time that I used my new union status to have an "Equity" audition. I felt a true sense of accomplishment to have the privileges it rendered. I think it was also probably my last audition in New York before I leave to return to New Trier. But it made it seem all the more that I am in the right place in my life.

*June 14, Monday.*
We had our first rehearsal for the Andrew Lloyd Webber concert tour last night and it was a little difficult to sit through. We rehearsed for four hours, during which time we sat doing nothing most of the time. The musical director was not prepared, and although I was patient most of the night, I started dreading taking this job. I know it

will work out fine, but I hate being in situations where people aren't professional. The talent was quite good and I like the cast members already.

*June 20, Sunday (the summer solstice).*
Some final reflections on my adventure.

I think one of the great things I've learned about myself in this yearlong endeavor is that I could have actually failed at the business. I left it in the spring of 1994 after having worked steadily for many years. The longest I was ever out of work was three months and that happened only once. I always felt that I could work and get a job if I needed one and that when I left, it was to pursue something else—teaching— not because I was forced to leave. But after having been here for a year and doing a significant number of auditions, I realized that consistent success was not necessarily something I would have ultimately achieved. This was a profound realization.

Had I moved to New York when I originally contemplated it (in 1993), I would have still had the physical prowess and skill to have been cast in probably a couple of Broadway shows. This would have been possible primarily because I was a triple-threat-type package with the added bonus of tumbling skills. At the time I left the business I had come close to being cast in the revival of *Grease*, had done a successful audition for the casting agency Johnson/Liff—which at the time was the biggest agency in NYC, casting *Miss Saigon*, *Les Miserables*, and all of the Lloyd Webber shows (*Sunset Boulevard, Phantom of the Opera, Cats, Aspects of Love*)—and had gotten called to come in to audition for the roles of Tumblebrutus and Macavity in *Cats* on Broadway. Several shows at the time required tumblers: *Damn Yankees, Cats, Beauty and the Beast, Miss Saigon,* and probably a few others that I can't recall. Although I was thirty-one at the time, I looked twenty-five, about the right age and look for most of the work on Broadway

Ten years later, Johnson/Liff was no more. The type and look I had ten years prior had matured to young dad. Although the physique was for all practical purposes the same, the prowess had slipped a little and the tumbling skills were gone. My voice has improved dramatically since the early nineties because of continued voice studies with three wonderful teachers and a master's recital. But I was never able to use it to put myself in a good enough light or to gain advantage with another casting agency like I had with Johnson/Liff. Lastly, the desire to do whatever it took to get the job had left me.

This leaves me to hypothesize a different scenario. Had I moved to NYC and worked in a couple of shows beginning in 1993 (probably tumbling), I would have done well for a short while, perhaps two or three years. In that time I would have made good money and lived well. However, the rigors of tumbling would have forced me, probably sooner rather than later, to quit that aspect of the business. Eventually, I would have needed to rely more on my singing and acting, and less on my dancing. I was never on a lead role track and I would have bounced from one chorus to another and had the frequent stint of unemployment. This would have brought me into my early forties, the same age as when I began my sabbatical, having the same young-dad look but with diminished physical skills, improved vocal skills, and a few more connections. I believe I would have gotten to a point where the incredibly difficult grind of show business would have left me to contemplate a different career or to resign myself to a life of inconsistent work and modest living.

I think I would have developed more quickly and intensely the already painful arthritis I have in my hips from the additional pounding from tumbling. I also can't imagine what might have happened in my relationships and social life. I would have missed out on owning a home and becoming a member of the wonderful community of Evanston. My future and eventual retirement would not have looked nearly so bright.

I also would have missed out on becoming a teacher at New Trier and all that that career has brought me. I think I would have become a good teacher, but my development was greatly enhanced by my relationships with all of the talented teachers in the music department and the rest of the New Trier faculty. I would have missed out on working with the talented students at New Trier and developing the relationships I covet with both students and staff in the New Trier community. I would have never led one of the finest high school music departments in the country. Lastly, I feel fortunate to work in an environment that encouraged my sabbatical leave so that I could grow in so many profound ways. I look forward to returning to New Trier and repaying my debt with inspired teaching and leadership.

*Afterword, June 30, 2011, Thursday.*
With the passage of time, I have reflected on my year in NY and on the final journal entries I made. I realized I left some stories unfinished and hadn't included culminating thoughts on the pursuit of my musical theatre career that could be of benefit to students.

After one rehearsal, the European tour scheduled for July and August of 2004 was abruptly canceled. Apparently, our production company hadn't gone through the proper channels to secure the rights to some of the material we were going to be performing, and the Really Useful Group, Andrew Lloyd Webber's production company, pulled the plug on the tour. Although Katherine and I were disappointed that we weren't able to do the tour, it did make life much easier for our transition back to our Evanston home and New Trier.

My year in New York was fruitful in that I was offered and participated in five projects (although the fifth, the Euro tour, was dramatically curtailed). *There's A Marquee...*, although lacking in production value, gave me an off-Broadway credit, provided me with (albeit meager) earnings (around $150) and a connection to the casting consultant Bob Luke. *Chess In Concert*, although nonpaying, was a rich experience. It offered high-quality production value, the opportunity to see and work with the very best, the star-studded aspect of the single-night New Amsterdam theatre performance, and the opportunity to have a Broadway credit on my resume. *The Kid Who Played the Palace* didn't pan out as I had originally hoped with a staged-reading performance opportunity and possibly more. Nonetheless, I participated in an original cast recording of a show that later went on to a world-premiere staged reading at the Emelin Theater, Mamaroneck, New York. Clearly the biggest opportunity was doing *Footloose* at Westchester Broadway Theatre, where I earned my Equity card, performed in a show for three months, and earned approximately $5,000.

All in all I did twenty-seven auditions, had three callbacks, and was offered roles in five projects. I earned approximately $5,150 plus some expenses. I spent $1,100 on my Equity card, approximately $800 ($16 x 50) for dance classes, $360 for six sessions of Paul Harmon's musical theatre audition technique class, $750 ($75 x 10) on voice lessons, and about $1,000 for a year's membership at the Y (for both Katherine and me).

Lance, the cat, flew back to Evanston with me July 31, 2004, and we both struggled through a sleepless first night in a strange environment (for me, a deafeningly quiet neighborhood; for Lance, a vaguely and oddly familiar house). During a checkup at the vet shortly before we left New York, we discovered that Lance was probably closer to seventeen years old. He passed away that September but only after happily readjusting to his old house and taking leisurely strolls in his reappropriated kingdom, our backyard.

Upon her return to Evanston, Katherine began a new life as a nonunion actress, director, and teacher. She gave up her union status in order to pursue roles that she wanted to play. Besides performing in three cabarets at Davenport's (a well-known, intimate cabaret venue in Chicago), she portrayed the Spider Woman in *Kiss of the Spider Woman*, Giulietta in *Aspects of Love*, Georgie in *The Full Monty*, Arlene in *Baby*, Mrs. Mullin in *Carousel*, and Norma Desmond in *Sunset Boulevard*. She has directed a staged reading of *Cowboy Versus Samurai* at Silk Road Theatre and *Feeding the Moonfish* at The Artistic Home. She is currently teaching acting at Actors' Training Center in Wilmette, Illinois.

At New Trier in August 2004, I once again assumed the roles of choral director and music department chair and continue doing so at this printing. In that span of time I returned to New York, with music department capstone ensembles Concert Choir and Symphony Orchestra, and conducted both in the Spotlight Ensemble Series at Carnegie Hall in April 2006. The New Trier music department was recognized by the GRAMMY Foundation as the 2007 National Grammy Signature School. In March 2012, three New Trier capstone ensembles will travel to Sydney, Australia, for an exchange with New Trier's sister city high school, Pittwater High School, and perform in the Sydney Opera House. My involvement with musical theatre continues as I direct the annual Choir-Opera musical. Since 2005 I have directed *The Music Man*, *Pippin*, *West Side Story*, *Guys and Dolls*, *Carousel*, *Thoroughly Modern Millie*, and *Les Misérables*. Production quality at New Trier is extraordinarily high because of a committed production team, generous resources, and eager and talented pupils. Many of my former students have gone on or continue to go into musical theatre training programs, and several have performed in Broadway shows and union and nonunion theatres around the country.

Since my last professional production (*Footloose*), I haven't performed except for the occasional solo at a friend's party or for my classes at New Trier. After taking voice lessons religiously for thirteen years, my technique finally improved to the point where I can maintain my voice without having to study. Although I could use a lesson from time to time to continue to develop my tenor range, I haven't felt motivated to do so with the little energy I have left after teaching and leading the department at New Trier. My days of choreographing the shows at New Trier finished after setting the dance numbers for *The Music Man* and *Pippin* (in Fosse style), although I still choreograph a number or two in our yearly Broadway revues.

For years after I stopped performing in the '90s, I still harbored the desire to perform in a Broadway show. When several of my peers did so with frequency, I realized it was an achievable goal. My career dreams in musical theatre felt complete, however, after the year in which I earned my Equity card and performed on Broadway in *Chess* (although it was only one performance). Taking the place of my self-oriented goals are new goals to help young people find and pursue their talents. I am passionate about directing the annual Choir-Opera musical and seeing more than 150 students (cast, crew, and orchestra) have a first-rate theatrical experience. When students venture courageously down that path toward a career in the footlights, I experience the excitement with them. I feel accomplishment knowing they are sweating in a dance class, working vocal technique with a teacher, or taking huge risks in an acting class. And I am fulfilled when I am sitting in a theatre about to watch a former student cross the proscenium and appear in his or her own footlight dreams.

# part three

## THE TEACHER'S COMPANION
## FOR *FOOTLIGHT DREAMS*

## WHY A TEACHER'S COMPANION?

After spending the better part of a year creating my guidebook for students and putting it into the hands of many, it became apparent that adding a teacher's companion could allow the information to reach even more people and become a more practical tool.

The guidebook is intended to help students make educated, conscious decisions about career choices. However, students who picked up the book were struggling with how to incorporate its information into their decision-making. To have a teacher guiding that process makes total sense.

My experience both as a working actor and as an educator can provide students, teachers, and parents with a significant amount of information. Making the right decisions about careers is still not foolproof, but I hope the combination of the Teacher's Companion, the guidebook, and the diary will help the student make a smart choice.

To teachers,

As you are fully aware, advising students (and parents) about a career in show business is full of pitfalls. I cannot count how many times parents have asked me, "Does my kid have what it takes to make it in the business?" This question cannot be answered!

When students come into your office and ask about careers, suggest that they read this book. Try to pinpoint their concerns. Most likely, their biggest fear is the uncertainty of being successful in the career itself.

Help them make an educated choice about A) whether or not to pursue a career in the business, and B) how to prepare for that career should they decide to pursue it.

Use this Teacher's Companion. By engaging the student in conversation through prompt-like questions, the following content will suggest ways in which you may want to use *Footlight Dreams*.

*David Ladd*

# SECTION A

## Using *Footlight Dreams* to help students determine whether to pursue a career in the musical theatre business.

### Read Part One, Section One: A Preposterous Idea, page 3

I never thought any of the book's opening quotes would scare a student away from contemplating a career in musical theatre, but I did hope that they might set in motion more serious thought. The quotes certainly can be used to start a discussion.

Ask the student:

- What is your initial impression of these quotes?

- Which ones stand out to you, both positively and negatively?

- Do you think any differently about a career now that you've read these quotes?

*When your students are wondering if they have what it takes…*
*Help them recall and clarify their passion moments.*

### Read Part One, Section Two: Exploring the Myth and Reality, pages 4 to 6

This part is devoted to the talent versus passion debate. When students ask "Do I have the talent?" or "Do you think I should give this a try?" (or, for that matter, when parents ask the same questions about their student), I have **never** said no. I do not believe it is my place to do so; students need to discover for themselves whether or not they can make it in this career. The last thing I want to see is a student looking back ten, fifteen, or twenty years from now and regretting that he or she didn't give it a go. By discussing talent and passion with the student, a teacher can help the student see the issue more clearly.

Recalling and clarifying their passion moments:

- Do you recall the moment or moments that inspired you to consider pursuing musical theatre? When was it? What were you doing? Describe it; share the details. What did you feel? Why was this moment so important?

Other important questions for the students to answer for themselves so they are more aware of the realities of the business:

- How do you deal with not being cast in the role you want?

- Why are you considering a career in this field? What motivates you?

- What do you see as your strengths?

- What types of roles do you see yourself playing in five, ten, or fifteen years from now?

*When your student (or a parent) is questioning the viability of a career in the biz…*

## Read Part One, Section Two: Exploring the Myth and Reality, pages 7 to 9

These pages try to cut through the "I love doing shows" mindset and get to a practical discussion. The section calls into play the passion aspect by very bluntly describing the business as difficult but doable. There is a little bit of dry information regarding becoming a union actor but it is all information that is valuable when deciding whether or not to pursue the career.

- Describe AEA.

- Why is it important?

- Describe the difference between union and nonunion theatre work.

- Are there union theatres in your city?

- In what city do you wish to pursue a career in musical theatre? Why?

- Create a comparison of musical theatre work in the cities of Chicago and New York City by describing the types of professional musical theatre jobs in each (regional dinner theatre, off-Broadway, etc.). (There isn't any mystery to this question. Chicago has a very limited number of union musical theatre houses, and much of New York is listed in any playbill of a Broadway or off-Broadway show.) Does each city fit your goals? Remember, you will be trying to make a living as a musical theatre professional.

- Would you consider commercial, television, and film work to supplement your musical theatre career? Which medium(s) interest you?

*When your student says, "I want to work only on Broadway!"*

## Read Part One, Section Two: Exploring the Myth and Reality, pages 14 to 15

Broadway is only one of **many** possible places for a musical theatre career. Most musical theatre actors in the United States are working not on Broadway but in national tours, regional theatres, and summer stock. It is great to have the drive and to go for Broadway, but try to help the student understand that the most important thing—at least for most people, eventually—is to work consistently and make a life of it. Explore the myth of the Broadway idea. This can help the student identify and reframe what else is possible. Another reality is that if he or she does not receive support from another source (parents, family, spouse), then it is more than likely that at some point a survival job will be required.

- Why Broadway? What does that mean to you?

- Where are the union theatres in your area?

- Have you seen shows at these theatres? What were your likes and dislikes?

- Look at the costs for moving to NYC (on pages 32 and 38). Will you be prepared financially?

*When your student contemplates skipping college to go straight into the business…*

## Read Part One, Section Two: Exploring the Myth and Reality, pages 9 to 13 and Part Two, Section One: When You Get There, pages 31 to 39

The examples in the book show many ways to start a career in the business. I believe the highest degree of success will be attained if a student enters a degree program that offers training for the exact career he or she wishes to pursue.

However, if a student is convinced that he or she is not going to go to college, give as much information as you can to guide the early part of the musical theatre career. Encourage the student to enter a two-year certificate program that provides musical theatre training and "street smarts" information on developing good business skills. If you can't persuade the student to do this, provide as much information as possible: A list of voice teachers, quality dance studios, and acting studios in his or her desired city. Training is crucial for two reasons: An actor has to continue to grow in skill in order to compete in the field, and training is a vehicle for making professional connections that can result in employment opportunity.

- Where will you go to study and grow your craft?

- What contacts have you made that will help get you work as an actor?

- How long can you subsist before taking a survival job?

- Do you have a friend with whom you can share living expenses?

- What tools will you use to assist with your trade?

## Take a trip to New York City.

I think the best advice for a student contemplating a career in musical theatre is to encourage a trip to New York City. It can often be the deciding factor that spurs the student on or helps the young person see that he or she really doesn't want to do it. This should not be a tourist trip but should be shaped in a way to provide a first professional experience.

- See shows (not just Broadway but off-Broadway and off-off).
- Try to meet actors after a show. Talk to them and ask them questions.
- Use public transportation (subway, primarily, or a cross-town bus).
- Check out the Actors' Equity Association office at 165 West Forty-sixth Street in Times Square. (You'll see sign-up boards for auditions there and an interesting atmosphere.)
- Attend an open call.
- Take a dance class at Broadway Dance Center, Steps, or Dance Space Center.
- Explore Lincoln Center Music Library.
- Explore the city. Take a Gray Line tour, walk through Central Park (make sure you have a map, and do it in daylight your first times), or check what's going on at NYU and Juilliard.
- Check out some real estate websites to find rental prices for apartments in different neighborhoods in Manhattan and the other boroughs.

There is a certain grittiness and harsh reality to experiencing New York in this way but it also is incredibly exciting and stimulating.

# SECTION B
## Using *Footlight Dreams* to help students prepare for a career in the business should they decide to pursue it.

*When a student has made up his or her mind to pursue musical theatre and asks, "What's next?"…*
### Read Part One, Section Three: School Selection, pages 16 to 21

It is incredibly important for the student to continue to train while he or she is applying to colleges. The student improves his or her skills and gains confidence in all endeavors such as continuing to audition for parts and shows at your school, for community productions, and, of course, for schools and scholarships. Lessons and classes also will get the students into the "training" mode, which is exactly what they'll be doing for the next four years. They should be shoring up their weaker skill sets.

- Are you taking voice lessons right now?

- Are you taking dance right now?

- Are you in an acting class right now?

- Have you taken audition or "business of the biz" classes?

- Are you attending theatrical productions?

- Are you reading plays?

- Are you listening to musical works?

If the answer to any of these questions is no, help the student bridge the gap.

Regarding school type: If it's musical theatre the student is set on pursuing, he or she should apply for musical theatre programs. There are so many programs from which to choose, but probably the most important thing is determining a preference for a broad education or a laser education. The university experience will provide that broad, balanced college atmosphere, whereas the conservatory experience will be a complete immersion. As long as the school has a good reputation, either experience is legitimate. It depends on how the student best works and lives.

- Do you have important interests outside of your musical theatre circle? If so, will the schools to which you apply offer these experiences as well?

Lastly, be sure to have your own copy of *Directory of Theatre Training Programs* (or one of the other guides I mentioned in Part One, Section 3) and become familiar with the website *schoolsfortheatre.com*. They are wonderful resources and don't require you to be the final word on school choices.

*When your student asks for assistance in the application or school-selection process…*

## Read Part One, Section Three: School Selection, pages 20 to 21

Visits to colleges and/or universities are the most important aspect of choosing a school. Encourage your students to visit each school to which they are considering application.

- What are important characteristics or qualities to look for in a school as you make your visits? (Make a list.)

- Are the facilities of high quality and do they offer a variety of training opportunities?

- Are the dormitories to your liking?

- Are they in close proximity to the training facilities?

- Is the school near a city where you can see professional theatre?

- What does the school think of its education? (A good question to ask while you are visiting.) What are its graduates doing?

- Is a professional theatre company affiliated with the university?

The other important aspect for the admission process is audition preparation. As soon as the students narrow down their choices, they should compile the audition requirements of all the schools and create a least common denominator list of those requirements. Rather than preparing for each school one at a time, prepare for them all at once and then practice those pieces over and over.

- What songs will you sing that cover all of the auditions you will be doing?

- What monologues will you use in your upcoming auditions?

- How will you go about preparing these materials? (Private instruction versus courses in or outside of school.)

If the students are preparing with help from private coaches and teachers, you will not have to worry about the details of their choices. However, if you are filling in some of these gaps, make sure they have contrasting songs and monologues. For songs, plan on an up-tempo piece, a ballad, and perhaps even a quirky character song. For monologues, prepare one comedic, one dramatic, and one classical, all from published plays. Encourage the student to visit the website of each college for which they plan to audition to find detailed information on requirements for auditions.

*When your student wants all the advice he or she can get!*

## Read Part One, Section Four: Down the Road…, pages 22 to 28

This is an FYI section that gives a little bit of perspective on several important topics: The inevitability of continued training, the sobering realities of the financial picture, how ethnicity plays a part in job availability, and the importance of making connections. It concludes with a little advice from the professionals and, finally, a summary to help bring clarity.

- How do you feel about the author's suggestion that you will need to continue to train even after you finish your college degree?

- How will you meet the financial demands of making a move and settling in a city? Will you have support from your family or will you need to work in order to save?

- Does the information about ethnicity change the way you view the business?

- What did you think of the information on the connections aspect of the business? What is your comfort level with the cultivation of these important relationships?

- There is some enlightening information in the "Advice from the pros" section. Did anything surprise or impress you?

- Have your thoughts about this career changed in any way?


*Finally, leaving no stone left unturned…*

## Encourage the student to read Part Two, Sections Two and Three (the journal preface and then the journal itself), and then spend some time reflecting with you afterward.

- What did you think of Mr. Ladd's year in New York?

- What surprised you?

- Was he focused on process or product?

- What do you think about doing auditions for auditions' sake?

- What did you think about the fact that his getting the job in three of his five experiences was at least in part because of his connections?

# SECTION C
## For Future Musical Theatre Performers

### Concepts for eighth- and ninth-graders

Quality musical theatre experiences are most important at this age. If these students have a lot of fun doing musical theatre and get excited about it, that is generally enough and they will pursue it with increasing vigor and passion. In my community, several community and children's theatres expose young people to the classics and give them performance opportunities. This is a terrific tradition and our community is richer because of it. When the students come to New Trier High School, they are experienced and trained performers and have a high expectation for their musical theatre experiences here.

Any kind of musical involvement—from playing an instrument to singing in a choir—is very advantageous to developing musical skills. Additionally, seeing professional (and amateur) productions of theatre, musical theatre, opera, and dance should also be a part of their experience, as they will enjoy these productions and see for themselves the viability of the work.

As your students begin to have quality experiences, and truly enjoy them, encourage them to add summer musical theatre activities. Many universities and summer music camps offer a variety of options. As your students continue to develop their passion and skills, mention that there are jobs out there! Tell them it is possible—with a lot of work, a lot of practicing, and a bit of good karma—to have a career doing what they love.

The most important thing is for them to get involved and have fun doing musical theatre.

It's never too early to start dreaming of a life among the footlights.

# ABOUT THE AUTHOR

David Ladd is a choral director and the Music Department chair at New Trier High School in Winnetka, Illinois, where he has taught since 1996. One of his teaching assignments is Choir-Opera, a ninety-voice group devoted to the study of musical theatre. Mr. Ladd received a Bachelor of Music degree from the University of Wisconsin–Madison, a Master of Music from Northeastern Illinois University, and a Master of Education from National-Louis University. Before his career in education, he was a professional actor in musical theatre. He performed in productions such as *Damn Yankees, 42nd Street, Me and My Girl, Carousel, Jesus Christ Superstar,* and *Cats,* as well as many revues in theme parks and on cruise ships. In 2003 he was granted a sabbatical to return to the profession of musical theatre and to pen the original concept of this book. In his year's leave he appeared on Broadway in The Actors Fund benefit of *Chess* and earned his Equity card while performing in a production of *Footloose* at Westchester Broadway Theatre.

## Chronology of Professional Musical Theatre Experience

The Kids From Wisconsin – June–August 1981

The Kids From Wisconsin – June–August 1982

Wisconsin Singers – August 1982–May 1983

*The Evolution of Rock*, Marriott's Great America – June–October 1983

*American Pop*, Marriott's Great America – July–October 1984

Boy Scouts of America 75th Anniversary Jamboree – September 1985

*America*, Stage Manager, Six Flags Great America – February–October 1986

*Bugs Bunny's Looney Tunes Parade*, Director/Choreographer, Six Flags Great America – June–July 1986

*Christmas Cabaret!* Classic Arts Dinner Theatre, Appleton, WI – November–December 1986

*Baby*, Danny, Village Playhouse of Wauwatosa, WI – January–March 1987

*Stars and Stripes Revue*, Stage Manager, Six Flags Great America – February–October 1987

Great America Marching Band, Director/Choreographer, Six Flags Great America – May–August 1987

*Merry Mardi Gras Parade*, Director/Choreographer, Six Flags Great America – June–July 1987

*South Pacific*, Music Under the Stars, Milwaukee, WI – July 1987

*La Traviata*, Assistant Director, Music Under the Stars, Milwaukee – August 1987

*And the Winner Is…*, Opryland – February–October 1988

*The General Jackson All-Star Revue*, Opryland – November–December 1988

*Way Out West*, Opryland – February–October 1989

*America's Honda*, Live Industrial, Grand Ole Opry House – September 1989

*The 23rd Annual Country Music Association Awards*, Grand Ole Opry House – October 1989

*Christmas Stories*, General Jackson, Opryland – November–December 1989

*42nd Street*, SS *Norway* – January–May 1990

*Sealegs Goes Hollywood*, SS *Norway* – January–May 1990

*Mame*, Music Theatre of Wichita (KS) – June 1990

*Carousel*, Music Theatre of Wichita – July 1990

*Jesus Christ Superstar*, Music Theatre of Wichita – July 1990

*Me and My Girl*, Music Theatre of Wichita – August 1990

*Spirit of America with Brenda Lee*, Opryland – September–October 1990

*Footloose*, Music Video, Japanese MTV – October 1990

Bridal Fashion Show, Industrial, Grand Ole Opry House – November 1990

*A Tennessee Christmas*, Opryland Hotel – November–December 1990

*Sherwin Williams 125 Years*, Industrial, Grand Ole Opry House – January 1991

*Damn Yankees*, Drury Lane Oakbrook (IL) – February–May 1991

*Distant Horizons, And That's Dancin', Broadway, Sophisticated Sorcery*, Royal Viking Line *Sun* – June–December 1991

*Chicago Hair Show*, Hyatt O'Hare Hotel – February 1992

*Musicals of the Silver Screen, What a Wonderful World, A Cole Porter Revue*, RVL *Queen* – April–June 1992

*Cats*, Zurich – July 1992–July 1993

*Cats*, Basel – December 1993 – February 1994

*There's A Marquee…*, American Theatre of Actors – August–September 2003

*Chess*, Actors Fund Benefit Concert, New Amsterdam Theatre – August–September 2003

*The Kid Who Played the Palace*, original concept recording – August–November 2003

*Footloose*, Westchester Broadway Theatre – February–May 2004